CW01627152

KISSING DAISY PARKER

MICHAEL MILTON

KENSETT BOOKS

First published in Great Britain in 2020

Paperback ISBN 9781838047412
eBook ISBN 9781838047405

Kensett Books
Unit 34883
PO Box 26965
Glasgow
G1 9BW

For Kiran.

I am here.

Whenever you are ready.

THREE IMAGINARY BOYS

TRACK 1: OBJECT

DAISY: First, they snap your jaw. Then they shave your bones and bolt metal plates into your face. Your head puffs up to three times its normal size, and the bruises make you look like you've boxed twelve rounds with Iron Mike Tyson. It hurts. You scream when the packing comes out of your nose. Oh, and there's the chance that the snapping, shaving and bolting of surgery won't work. Psychological support? Zero. Nobody to help you process looking in the mirror at a totally different person. You were on a waiting list for months, in braces for two and a half years, and knew all along that this was coming. But nothing can prepare you. After seventeen years of looking at it in the mirror, the face on that person called "you" is gone.

Would I recommend it?

Definitely.

My profile's no longer a waning crescent moon, my thin nose has widened, and my bottom teeth finally sit behind the top. My new jawline means no more:

"Daisy's chin is so big it has its own postcode."

No more:

"When Daisy entered the Big Chin Olympics they said 'sorry, no professionals'."

No more:

"When Daisy fell and her chin hit the ground, I didn't laugh, but the pavement cracked up."

Double jaw surgery for a class three underbite is no fairy-tale. But it's better than going through life hearing every "yo momma" joke turned into a "Daisy's chin" joke. I do look better; pretty, even. I never thought I cared about that stuff. Turns out I do.

Eight months on and my face is still adjusting to its new shape, going through subtle changes week to week. People focus on the aesthetics, but I'm still retraining my jaw muscles. I thought that once my bottom teeth sat behind the top, I'd be able to indulge my sense of taste. Nope. I've actually lost a chunk of weight 'cause I can't be bothered chewing food. I can crunch into an apple for the first time in my life, but don't expect me to finish the thing. It's too much work. Another side effect is a permanent numbness in the lower left part of my face (heightening my ever-so-ladylike habit of sleep-drooling). You wouldn't notice it though, even now I've told you it's there.

Is it weird?

I suppose so, but my entire head's a different shape, so everything feels weird. I've got used to the numbness the same way I've got used to everything else. To eating and drinking and brushing my teeth.

Kissing?

Well, that's flipped on its head. To be honest, the new Daisy isn't used to kissing the old Greg, but between you and me, that's got nothing to do with my jawline.

JUNAID: *Destroy the image, and you will break the enemy.*

Bruce Lee, claw marks across his face and torso, stalks the evil Mr Han in the room of mirrors. Mirrors which play tricks on the senses. Mirrors which make their epic fight as much a battle of wits as it is of physical prowess. But when those words of wisdom come to him, Bruce knows what to do. He smashes the mirrors one by one, allowing him, finally, to defeat his nemesis. Delivering his patented running side kick, Bruce impales Mr Han on a spear and saves the day. The immortal scene comes from *Enter the Dragon,* the film that made Bruce a global superstar.

I re-enact it in my bathroom.

First, I touch my toothpaste "claw marks" and taste my own "blood". Next, I deliver (fake) blows to the cabinet doors and the shaving mirror above the sink. Then I'm on the landing, and I Bruce-Lee-running-side-kick a pillow I've stuck in the laundry basket.

'WWAAAAZZZAAAAAAAAAAHHHHHHHHH!'

I first watched *Enter the Dragon* on the 24th of April 1986. I remember because it was my tenth birthday. Eight years later, I'm officially an adult. Supposedly a man. But I'm still kung-fu kicking pillows with toothpaste on my chest. Usually, it's "Mr Han" who flies to his death against my bedroom door. But it's not Mr Han I kick today; it's Greg. I boot my best friend from one side of the landing to the other, because Daisy is all I can think about since she became, you know...*sexy*. I never thought I cared about appearances. Turns out I do.

In the shower, I daydream about the upcoming summer in Australia, a trip to celebrate Daisy's eighteenth and the end of school forever. I imagine Greg being eaten by a crocodile in the wilderness, leaving Daize and me mourning together in a log cabin. The outback's so hot that we grieve in our underwear, and there's only so long we can wait before touching each other's sticky bodies...

I wash my guilt down the plughole with the toothpaste. And, having just fantasised about his crocodiley demise, I need to look Greg in the eye at the bus stop.

Happy Birthday, Junaid.

GREGOR: I take it you've heard about Daisy's jaw? I can tell by the look on J's face that he's mentioned it. No doubt he said how my cute little underbiter now looks like the cover of *Vogue* magazine. It was months ago, but everyone at school still goes on and on about how great she looks. "Ooooh, I can't believe the difference" and "she looks like a new person" and "I can't stop looking at her" and blah blah blah. Dickbags. Half of these people didn't even speak to her before the operation. If I'd a penny for every ugly duckling to beautiful swan reference, I'd have enough cash to fly us all to Oz and back. I never thought I'd care about the effects of the surgery. Turns out I do.

I know what you're thinking. You're thinking, who *doesn't* want their ugly duckling to turn into a beautiful swan? But here's the thing: Daize was always a swan to me. So those ugly duckling comments are offensive. I've told Daisy this, and she says it's "sweet". Sweet! Is it sweet that she gets sex-eyed by everyone whose path we cross? Guys staring in the corridors, girls lingering in the changing rooms, Miss Dupont the French teacher ogling in the canteen. Worst of all, is it sweet that my best pal looks at her that way? Aye, Junaid Jarvis, that means you. Sat next to me on the bus, gibbering about how he woke up early to watch the mirror scene from *Enter the Dragon*. As if he wasn't actually fantasising about my girlfriend. J, who called Daisy "Judge Dredd" when we first got together, because her chin was such a "feature". Is that sweet? Is it?

I didn't ask for this. This is not part of the Master Plan. How am I supposed to practise for the *Scottish Street Fighter II*

Championships when I'm too busy looking over my shoulder for Don Juans? Duckling to swan is one thing, but let me ask you this: who wants their perfectly-formed beautiful swan to turn into a cover model?

Nobody. That's who.

TRACK 2: 10:15 SATURDAY NIGHT

DAISY: It's a red-sky-at-night-shepherd's-delight evening. I flick through my pile of holiday brochures while listening to the underwateryness of 'Plainsong' from the Cure's 1989 album, *Disintegration*. Greg's CD player, my CD. Lumpy the dachshund lies asleep at my feet, and Greg's in his "gaming chair". Grungy hair brushes his thick shoulders. His beard's so grown out it looks like a Viking is hunched over the control pad. He's focussed on practising for his *Street Fighter* Championships to the point that he's forgotten I'm in the room. The annual competition defines his very soul. I sometimes get annoyed at Greg paying more attention to pixelated princesses than he does to me. And yet, the lame plastic trophy is offset by the fifteen-hundred quid cash prize for the winner. No doubt, he needs it in his Australia fund.

The trophies from the previous three years have their very own shelf, separate from the nerd's paradise around them. Figurines of Samurai babes with swords, ninja stars, and impossible cleavage are on top of a bookcase full of fantasy novels and manga comics translated from Japanese. He reads these in the lavvy. Another shelf has every console and computer he's ever owned, boxed and in mint condition. From left to right, top to bottom: Sinclair ZX Spectrum, Commodore 64, Nintendo Entertainment System, Sega Master System, Sega Megadrive, Neo Geo, Phillips CDi, Atari Jaguar, Sega Megadrive 2, Sega Mega CD 2 and a Panasonic 3DO. He's paid out hundreds of pounds for some of these, and all he does is play bloody *Street Fighter*.

If every one of the consoles was two hundred quid, then this shelf is over two grands' worth of machines. That's not counting any games or the fact that the 3DO alone was closer to five hundred. *Five hundred quid* for something he's barely touched. It's not that I don't support Greg in his passions. I do. But this specific passion is expensive.

Where does he get the money?

Same place he gets his ginger hair, his mam. Greg's the baby of the family and to say he's spoiled would be an understatement. His brothers are as bad as his mam for doing it. There're ten years between him and Kev, twelve between him and John. Both brothers and his dad all work offshore, so money isn't exactly scarce. I don't say that to be mean. In the four years I've been with Greg, his family has spoiled me too. I dunno. I could be worrying about nothing.

We're supposed to be going to Australia in the summer. Our first proper holiday on our own, like real adults. Grown-ups celebrating exams being over forever (well, till we go to uni). A once-in-a-lifetime trip to the other side of the world. It's three months away. He should be booking flights and saving cash. Not Greg. Oh no. He blows every penny on bits of plastic that he never uses and is more concerned with beating up fictional characters and their fictional haircuts in *Street Fighter*.

I look at the brochure again. At what an extra two grand could get me. Think about how rich I'd be once my pounds were more than doubled when converted to Aussie Dollars.

'Greg?' I'm ignored. 'Greg?' Still ignored. 'Greg. Greg. Greg. Greg. Greg. Greg. Greg. Greg. Gre–'

'Whaaaaat?'

I scratch Lumpy's ear.

'How much money have you saved for Australia?'

'Eh? Oh. I'm not sure. I'd need to check.'

'A grand?'

'Ha! That'd be–' he pauses his precious game to look at my face. '–Aye. Oh aye. Definitely more than a grand by now.' He switches into a crap Australian accent, unpauses and turns away, unable to look me in the eyes. 'I reckon, mate. Ah yea me ol' possum, me kaengeroooo, me kowahlee baer.' This is the kind of thing I've to put up with when he's trying to avoid answering a difficult question. The boy can be an idiot sometimes.

I open the drawer of Greg's bedside cabinet. He keeps his bank book in here, though it's a post office savings account, so it's not a real bank. I look inside and find that he's recently cleaned it out. A single pound remains. I leap from the bed and hit reset on the Super Nintendo, a fire in my stomach.

'Daize, for Christ's sake I'm in the middle o–' he notices the bank book, jumping from his chair to try and grab it. I hold it above my head.

'Last withdrawal, £1, 328. This better be some kind of joke, Gregor Buchan!' His face goes beetroot, but he doesn't say anything. 'Well…?'

'It's my money, Daize. I can spend it how I like.' He says it feebly, a naughty child caught with his hand in the biscuit tin.

'What about Australia? Who's going to pay for you to grace us with your presence there, Greg? Cause I'll tell you something for nothing, it won't be me. Come summer, I'm off, whether you're coming or not.'

'Calm down, Daize. I'll have plenty. The competition, remember? That's fifteen hundred quid in the bank, plus the next few months' wages. And I'm sure my brothers will give me a few quid holiday money. I'll have loads for Australia.'

'And what if somebody else wins the competition? Did you think about that?' The question hurts him, and I feel guilty asking, but it's a fair point.

'Nobody else is going to win. I'm number one, Daize.' He points at his trophies. 'Three years in a row, remember? But that's why I need to practise, I need to make sure.'

'We need that prize money, Greg. It's about more than some stupid plastic trophy this year, so you bloody well better make sure!'

JUNAID: It was a red-sky-at-night-shepherd's-delight evening on the 24th of April 1986. The night I first watched *Enter the Dragon*. Before Greg knew Daisy existed, before we had part-time jobs at ScotMart, before we went to Invergowan Academy and had to get a bus to school. Orange fire burned in the clouds. The Easter holidays crept by lazily. My birthday treat was an afternoon spent with mum, dad and Greg in the swimming pool, but now Greg and I stood alone in the empty swing park.

'Where is everyone?' asked Greg. I didn't know where everyone was, and I also didn't know that I was about to have my first-ever fight.

Heads poked out of a bush. Then, a body sprinted towards me.

'You're dead!' It was Beezer, the chubbiest kid from my class at school. I bolted, and Beezer chased. Adrenaline rose up the front of my body, but a second or two into my sprint, I stopped. I thought, *no, I'm not having this. I'm not fighting. He* was nearby. Skud. My nemesis. I could feel his eyes on me, but I didn't care. I wouldn't do it. I'd never had an issue with Beezer, but Skud had turned him and every other kid in the village (except Greg) against me. Why else would Beezer storm out of the bushes to challenge me to a death match? I spun around to face him.

'What have I ever done to you?' Beezer's face wobbled with fear. He was scared too. He hadn't expected me to stop and it was clear he didn't want to fight either.

'What d'you mean?' he asked. I'd been to Beezer's house. His mum's a nurse, and she'd put a plaster on my knee after I'd skinned it in the street outside. She poured me a glass of Coke and made me sit down till I finished it.

Before Beezer or I could think about the situation for too long, there he was. Commanding his army from atop a wall, jutting out his bottom teeth like Jaws from the *James Bond* films:

Skud.

Full-lipped, black-haired, blue-eyed, muscle-toned and Hollywood-toothed. Skud was an incomer to the village who ruptured the status quo. There was this face he pulled in the midst of evil. He'd push his tongue into his bottom lip: half focus, half pleasure. I was terrified of seeing that face. It was the face I imagined on serial killers as they learned their trade on the neighbourhood cats. I doubted he'd end up a serial killer, but he was often in trouble at school, prompting my mum to label him an "PTBA" (Prat To Be Avoided). He jumped down from the wall and strolled over with an arrogant bounce in his step. He knew that he was one running side kick from a death match victory.

'It's a joke, Pinglish.' I *despised* the nickname. My dad was raised in Kent where he met my English mum (and her Pakistani parents). The two of them moved up here after their marriage saw my mum disowned. Dad got the chance to work at his uncle's business, and they jumped at the opportunity to live by the sea. I was born right here. I've never been to Pakistan, don't speak more than a few words of Urdu, and did not meet my grandparents before they passed away. While I have my mum's south Asian skin and my parents' south English accent, our tiny Scottish fishing village, Cairn Bay, is the only place I know. "Pinglish" is supposed to be funny. It isn't.

'I'm Scottish.'

Skud flicked his hand to move Beezer out of the way. 'I know. We're mucking about; nobody wants a fight here.' Always lies, effortless lies. He came towards me with his arm outstretched, offering a handshake. A reptile approaching an insect. Greg was at my side and put up his arm to stop me. Greg is short, but he was stockier than the rest of us. I swear he could've grown a full beard at ten years old if he'd thought about it.

'Don't do it.' Greg's eyes locked on Skud, ready to come to my rescue. But it was too late. Despite everything in my body telling me to bolt, my legs were numb. I *knew* he wanted to hurt me. He'd take pleasure in humiliating me with his reptile smile and pokey-out lip. But still, I extended my hand, desperate to believe that we could all be friends. One of the heads in the bush shouted:

'It's a trap!'

Half a dozen boys from my class tumbled out and ran to get close to the action. Skud clenched my hand and tugged me towards him, at the same time throwing a roundhouse kick at my left leg. I turned into it, and it landed on my backside. It didn't hurt at all. I ragged my hand out from his grip, pulling so hard that I fell to my hands and knees. Skud winded me with another kick, this time in my chest. Then Greg hit him in the face as if it was nothing. One punch and Skud went down. By that point, I was up, running as fast as I could and struggling to inhale.

From the ground, Skud shouted after me:

'Run back to your mammy!' I stole a glance over my shoulder. Skud, still floored, held a hand over his eye as Greg ambled away casually.

When Greg caught up, he asked me why I didn't fight. The reason is simple; I was scared. But I didn't want to tell Greg that, so I looked at the ground instead. I'd done three years of Karate by then, but it was Greg who stood up for me, unafraid of getting hit.

'Don't worry,' he said, 'I know a film.' If you knew Greg, you'd understand that this meant he knew of a film that would inspire me to stand up for myself. *Enter the Dragon* came from his brother's collection. And Greg had no idea how much of an effect this movie would have on me. I was so mesmerised by Bruce Lee's screen presence that I joined the library. I got them to order every book they could find on him and his life.

I convinced myself that my history wasn't so different from Bruce's. Born in San Francisco but raised in Hong Kong, his skin was almost the same colour as mine. His English also had the "wrong" accent. He experienced racism in America and was typecast as a stereotypical "Asian". But he fought against it. Bruce refused the labels, refused to be pigeonholed as anything other than himself. He was American, he was Chinese, he was a bona fide arse kicker. Bruce fought to the death in a way I never could. Not with Skud, not with anyone. The stuff with Skud was so long ago, it shouldn't matter anymore, but here I am thinking about it. It still matters. *He* still matters. Eight years and a black belt later, I'm avoiding confrontations like my ten-year-old self. Especially the big ones.

And so that's my plan for the future. The same then as it is now: to stand up for myself. But that's easier said than done, isn't it? I tried on the bus on the way in, I tried at school, and I tried on the bus on the way home again. But I couldn't even tell my best friend that he'd forgotten my birthday.

GREGOR: It was a red-sky-at-night-shepherd's-delight evening when I won the inaugural *Street Fighter II* tournament. That was four years ago. What a night. I became a minor celebrity at school and was interviewed for the *Invergowan Herald*. "LOCAL BOY BECOMES NATIONAL CHAMPION." I knew then that gaming would be part of my life forever. But try explaining that to Daisy. We spent all evening arguing about my bank account.

She goes on and on about how J has saved more money than the two of us combined. And she's right, he's loaded. He must have five, maybe even six grand in the bank. But Daisy's sudden obsession with J and the state of his finances is missing the point.

Don't get me wrong. I've known J as long as I've known myself. He's my best friend. When I think back on childhood, there're few memories without J in them. Birthday parties and scraped knees. My first game console and staying up all night to play it. Fighting and making up a million times. Laughing. Loads of laughing. We slogged through primary and secondary school together and have seen each other almost every day since we were four years old. So, aye, J's my best pal. Aye, he's saved more money than I have. But he's a follower, not a leader. Think about it:

1/. I apply to Aberdeen Uni; J applies to Aberdeen Uni. (It was my idea, but still).

2/. I get a job at ScotMart; J gets a job at ScotMart. (I got him the gig, but still).

And now:

3/. I go with my girlfriend to Australia; J goes with my girlfriend (and me) to Australia. (We invited him, but still).

He might have more money than I do, but that's 'cause he plays it safe. Champions don't play it safe. They have to take risks. That's why I had to empty my bank account for a VX0 Virtual Reality helmet and the PC components to code it. It's all part of the Master Plan. And any Master Plan worth its salt needs a little outlay up front. Speculate to accumulate.

Neither J nor Daize have Master Plans.

Mine is as follows:

I'm about to win my fourth *Scottish Street Fighter II Championship* in a row. That's a given. I didn't say anything when J also decided to enter the competition this year. If he wants to make a fool of himself, then it's none of my business. After that, we get school and exams out of the way over the coming months.

At that point, the winnings and whatever I can save in between will be enough for Australia. I'll go over there with my cover model girlfriend, Daisy-P, and best bud, Junaid Jarvis. We'll celebrate Daisy's birthday with kangaroo burgers and Aussie beer. And if there're any gaming competitions, I'll become a national champion on a second continent. Gaming for a living isn't an option at this point in humanity, so when we return, I'm off to Uni. I'll get my degree in computing while coding software for the VX0 Virtual Reality helmet. After graduation, I'll flog the software for millions, marry Daisy, and make a comeback on the gaming scene.

I'll start my very own international competition, fly in the best guys from the USA and Japan, and beat them all. This'll seal my reputation as the greatest gamer on the face of planet Earth. Daize and I will have a litter of ginger swans who may or may not need underbite surgery. We'll raise the brood on technology in a mansion I'll build across the road from my mam and dad's house. I'll game all day, Daize can write her novels and do her journalism. If J doesn't figure out what to do with himself, he can live in a granny annexe above the garage and babysit the children. That's my plan for the future.

The *Master Plan*.

Not bad, eh?

DAISY: There's this bit in *The Bell Jar* when the main character (who we all know is Sylvia Plath) compares the future to a fig tree. I reread that part a lot. She's under this huge tree, and each fig represents a different life. One fig is her being a famous poet, and another is her having a traditional family with a husband and kids. There's a fig that's her becoming a university professor and another that's foreign travel. One even represents being an Olympic gold medallist rower. She wants all of them. Every single fig on the tree. Thing is, she's sure that choosing one fig means that the others'll disappear forever. And she can't decide. So the figs start to turn black and drop off the tree, and she's left there watching her potential lives slip away.

I have my own fig tree, but my figs aren't that different from Sylvia's. There's the same range of options to choose from, but how can you pick only one when they're all bright and brilliant in your imagination? Perfect, unlived, fantasy lives. You get close to one of them, and it makes the others look bigger, tastier. You move to them and guess what happens? The fig you left behind becomes the juiciest on the tree. So how can you be sure? If you pick one, then what happens to the others? Do they turn black and drop off, and you lose the chance of them forever?

Right now, I'm reaching for a fig that's Australia.

That's my plan for the future.

Beyond that?

No idea.

TRACK 3: ACCURACY

JUNAID: 'I'm Ryu.' That was Greg.

'You're Ken.' Me. We whisper-shout our argument in Daisy's music room as we fold up the bedding. Greg slams a rolled-up sleeping bag onto the floor.

'I'm the reigning, soon-to-be four-time champion. I'm not having my picture taken dressed as a character I don't play.' I'm entering the *Street Fighter II Championships* along with Greg this year. I won't win, but it's doing a good job of winding him up. We're still arguing about who gets to be Ryu, the character we both use when playing. We'd gone to sleep having this argument, and we've woken up having this argument.

Daisy's mum, Grace, doesn't let Greg sleep in the same room as Daize despite them being over the legal age of consent. This predicament means that at 2 AM, Greg disappears into Daisy's bedroom across the hall. Grace sleeps in a room at the back of the house, which is downstairs and actually used to be Daisy's room, but–never mind. It's complicated. The point is that when I stay over at Daisy's house, I'm forced to listen to the unmistakable sound of Greg-and-Daisy sex. Daisy's moans are higher pitched than you'd imagine from someone who's spent her teens wearing Doc Martens. Greg, exactly as you'd expect, is silent but for a final grunt. Which is how intercourse must sound with *The Terminator*.

Does it *upset* me to listen to them?

"Upset" isn't the right word. Initially, I was fascinated because I'd never heard anyone at it before. Then it made me jealous, hearing Greg in his post-sex bliss. He'd stumble back into the room, roll into his sleeping bag and snore like a smug ginger Buddha. Mostly, though, it makes me feel left out that they have this secret I'm not allowed to be part of. That sounds like I want a threesome. I *definitely don't*. It's more that having to listen to them do it makes me feel...*lonely*.

But there was no unification last night. Greg was too busy huffing and puffing over *Street Fighter* with the sound on mute. Daisy's given him one of her trademark ultimatums, though this one seems a little more severe than usual. It could be her time of the month. That would make sense. Daisy's PMT spreads to each of us, so we all become moody bastards.

'Ken is a white American with long blonde hair. You're a white Scotsman with long ginger hair. Ryu is an olive Asian with short black hair. I'm an olive Scots-Asian with short black hair. Ergo, GREGOR: You're Ken, I'm Ryu.'

'Don't pull the race card on *me*, dickbag. Looks have nothing to do with it. If it was down to looks, I'd paint myself green and go as Blanka. But I don't play Blanka, I play Ryu, and the whole point is to dress as the character you play.'

'I don't play Ken either.'

'Fine. We'll get another karate suit and both go as Ryu.'

'It's called a *gi*. And both these gis are mine: another reason *I* get to be Ryu.'

'Nobody's getting another bloody gi!' A sleepy semi-shout from Daisy at the door. Shapely pins with smooth shins extend from her oversized Robert Smith t-shirt. It might be the only thing she's wearing. Her tousled hair is scraped back from her glorious new face. 'Greg, your mam spent ages dying that thing red and doing the armholes to make the rips look authentic. One of you is going to wear it, and he's going to appreciate it.'

'I know, babe. J's wearing it.'

'I'm not wearing it.'

'Oh, for Christ's sake, you're like a pair of grumpy bairns. I'm tossing a coin.' She holds out her hand until one of us can come up with some money. Greg looks at me. I roll my eyes, fish into my pockets, and give her a pound. 'Heads, Greg wears the red one; tails, J wears it.'

'Wait a minute,' Greg butts in, 'it always comes up heads.'

'Fine, heads J wears the red one.'

'Wait,' I start, but I get a look that tells me not to finish the thought. Daisy flips the coin, catches it in its mid-air spin and slaps it on the back of her hand.

DAISY: A seagull thumps full-speed into the window of the bus, making the woman in front jump right into the aisle. The gull craps all down the glass before it manages to change course. I hope it's not an omen of the weekend to come. Greg's already in a huff after losing a coin flip to decide which colour of karate suit he'll wear at the competition. J's elected to sit five rows back from us. I listen to 'Doing the Unstuck' from the Cure's 1992 album, *Wish*, in my headphones. When the song finishes, Greg's got out his control pad, so I move next to J. I give him a nudge and offer him a breath mint, an old in-joke we have. He rolls his eyes and asks why I've moved seats.

'Greg's doing my head in.'

'Snoring?'

'Huffing, practising combinations, and visualising winning

the tournament.' J stands up for a peek at Greg's thumbs doing "combos" on the controller. He drops back into his seat.

'Jesus,' he says. 'He's brought a control pad with him. I sometimes think he takes it all a bit *too* seriously. No wonder he wins every year.' I know Greg'll win again this year; he *has to*. Though somewhere in my grumpy bitch state, I also want him to lose. Not in a mean way, but so that he finally learns his lesson about being more responsible with money. I can't say that to J, so I change the subject to the *Discovery*, an old wooden ship moored in Dundee.

'Did you see the *Discovery*? Imagine sailing the world in one of those. Being far out at sea, in the crow's nest on top of the mast, and there's nothing around you but water. And when it gets dark, all you can see and hear is black and waves sucking and slopping on the side of the boat.' J sits back in his chair and stares outside. The cold sky's a hundred shades of blue-grey. The bus smells like custard. When I first got together with Greg, I was two inches shorter, had bird's nest hair and a lack of major jaw surgery. J treated me more like an annoying little sister than a friend. Post surgery, everything's changed.

I touch my right leg to his left, nonchalant. When our legs make contact, his face goes beetroot. I'd be lying if I said I wasn't enjoying that purple fizzer of his. I lean my head on his shoulder and slip my right arm under his left. His heart does jumping jacks, and he crosses his legs.

Who's "Judge *Dredd*" now, Mr Jarvis?

GREGOR: After the fiasco which is checking into the B&B, we go straight to the Cellar, a pub near Charing Cross. This is the home of the *Scottish Street Fighter II Championships*. The inside of the Cellar is so dark that it's like stepping into an arcade. A board on the wall behind the horseshoe-shaped bar displays the cocktails *du jour*. They're all named after films.

There's the "Taxi Driver", the "Space Odyssey" and "The Shining". This is floor one. The next floor down is called the "Dungeon", where the events happen. The deepest floor down is the "Depths", where the toilets are. Three championships, three victories, three years I've been coming to the Cellar. It's still the coolest pub in the known universe. Nobody's up here on the top floor, because the action takes place down in the Dungeon.

The Dungeon's a gaming paradise filled with the familiar tunes of the *Street Fighter* stages. A hive of video game brethren is squished into the long, thin basement. TVs and sofas line each side of the room. People're crushed between the sofas, cheering on their pals. I start to feel better. I'm home.

There're usually three screens down here, but today there's a dozen for the competition. Most are 27-inch Sharp TVs: good TVs and a nice size for gaming, but my eyes are drawn to the monster at the back. Perched on a wee stage is a 45-inch Zenith. In the queue to sign up, I hear that it's for the semis and the final. Daisy nods towards it.

'That's the biggest TV I've ever seen. Imagine having that in your living room.' It's the first words anybody has said since we checked into the B&B and had to speak to the receptionist. I give a sympathetic smile.

'We'll all have TVs that size in our living rooms one day, Daize. And they'll be so thin they fit on the wall.' Daize and J look at each other and roll their eyes.

'Must be worth a fortune,' says J.

'It's a beauty, isn't it?' says a staff guy with a *Street Fighter* t-shirt and hair that covers his eyes. 'Nightmare getting it down the stairs, right enough.' He's at the table by the entrance, smoking. He gives Daisy sex-eyes through his fringe. 'You thinking about competing, sweetheart?'

I pull Daisy behind me.

'She's got a name, and she's got a boyfriend.' Daisy's jaw drops.

'Greg!'

Fringy starts to backtrack.

'Sorry, mate. I didn't mean–'

'I know exactly what you meant.' Aye. Look all you want, buddy. I'm the chosen one. She picked me.

I lift a pen from the table and fill in a sign-up form.

Daisy puts her huffy face back on and makes a beeline for the bar. Great, that's another fight to look forward to. I try to keep focussed and follow J to the downstairs lavvies to put the gis on. He ploughs through the crowd before I do, and by the time I get in there, he's got the white gi out of the bag. I've no idea what's come over me, but I grab the gi off him:

'You don't even *like* video games for Christ's sake. Gimme the white one.'

He grabs it back.

'I've been eighteen for three days. This trip is for me too, remember? Oh, no, that's right. You don't remember, because all you give a crap about is the colour palette of the pixelated version of yourself, you self-obsessed, ginger wanker!'

Bollocks.

Now his blabbering on the bus the other day makes sense. He always does the Bruce Lee thing on the morning of his birthday. I'm losing it. I forgot his eighteenth, made him turn his karate gis into costumes *and* hijacked his room at the B&B. I start apologising, but he throws the white gi in my face and then the red one for good measure. And as the lavvy door closes behind him, everything rushes through my head. Blowing the Australia money, fighting with my girlfriend, screwing everything up if I don't win this championship. To top it all off, I start a fight with my best pal. Over some karate pyjamas. What the hell am I doing?

JUNAID: We go downstairs to the toilets to put the gis on. Not that I'm into any of it after four hours grumping on the bus and then discovering I have to share my room at the B&B. Greg's been jittery for the last few days, but he transitions to a whole new level of asswipe as we move to get suited up. He starts mumbling, almost to himself, then things get weird pretty quick.

'I'm going to win, J. I need the money. I have to win.'

I don't say anything. I wait to see where he's going with this. Then he's being more forceful and directing his words at me. 'And I'm going to win in the white gi. I can't explain, but I need the white gi to win this year.'

He sounds like a lunatic.

'Greg, you use your fingers to play the game.'

'Aye, but if I can–I want the white one, J.'

'What about what *I* want?'

He grabs my hoodie and pushes me back against the wall.

'You don't even *like* video games for Christ's sake. Gimme the white one.'

I'm so taken aback that I can't retaliate. Greg's never done anything like this, ever. Letting go, he turns away:

'Sorry. I don't know what I, I just–'

I've got the gis out of the bag before he can continue, and I throw them in his face.

'Wear both of them.'

I slam the door as I leave the bathroom. Upstairs, Daisy's eyebrows rise in a question mark as she watches me leave the pub. As soon as I'm out of the door, I wonder: what the hell am I doing?

DAISY: If you're going to be Greg Buchan's girlfriend, there're a few things you should be aware of. First up, video games are number one. That can be hard to deal with. But they're not just above you, they're above human beings in general.

Number two is that a few times a year, you've to tag along to conventions and competitions that he wastes his money on. The conventions aren't so bad, I'll give him that. We've been to Edinburgh twice, and I've had my share of geeky fun dressing up and parading about. The expos have ice cream stalls, an improved female to male ratio, and more of a carnival atmosphere. But other meetups, like this one, are in dingy, smelly pubs full of unwashed bedroom dwellers. One comp in Dundee was in a guy's living room, windows sealed, dirty laundry strewn about on the floor. These competitions also happen in Manchester, in London, even in Paris. But Greg's world barely reaches the outskirts of Cairn Bay, let alone beyond the borders of Scotland.

In the early days, we travelled to these competitions with his brothers. They'd drive us down and back in the same day, stopping in greasy spoons on the A90 for all-day breakfasts. This is our first expedition on our own, and the first with the addition of J. It's supposed to be fun. We're alone in a far away city, the boys can get drunk legally now, and I have a fake ID that works. But Greg was a moody nightmare the whole way down on the bus. Next, I discover that J's giving up his bed in the B&B for us and sleeping on the floor cause Greg had to cancel our room last minute. (The whole one-pound-in-my-bank-account thing). And to top it all off, we get to the pub, and he turns into a macho nut job, making a tit of himself with the sign-up guy for, you know, asking if I wanted to sign up. I just know things are going to get worse.

I'm in a craphole pub in Glasgow, and I want to be in London or Manchester or Paris. I want to be in Australia. I want to be anywhere. School's over in a few months. We should be planning our escape from this country.

I use my fake ID to order a glass of "Space Odyssey". I pull the straw from the drink, drop it on the bar, and gulp down half the cocktail in one go. It numbs the senses to the smell of pubescent boys. As I finish my first glass, I see J storm out of the building. I think about following him, but that would cause more grief, so I order another cocktail instead. I dump the second straw next to the first, and a question pops into my head: what the hell am I doing?

SEVENTEEN SECONDS

TRACK 4: THREE

JUNAID: Coming from the darkness of the Cellar into the daylight is like going through a time slip. It's only three in the afternoon, but being in the dark pub has given the world a nighttime feel. The sky's overcast with grey. Wind curls around my limbs, and the first spits of rain land on my forehead. I'm thankful for my jeans and hoodie, not exactly waterproof, but not a karate gi with the arms ripped off either. I turn south and head towards the river Clyde.

Looming red brick buildings become railway arches. The rain's off, but the sky's still dark, and the clouds come down around me. I walk under the railway bridge and along Buchanan Street, turning at St. Enoch shopping centre. My uncle told me all about the shipbuilding that took place down at the river. Nuclear submarines come in and out here: 'subs that could wipe out continents,' he says. When the Clyde comes into view, the water mirrors the grey of the sky. Grey dock cranes amongst grey buildings with grey boats fastened to the river's sides. Grey, grey, grey. Like gone-off meat.

A little further up the street, a vast suspension bridge crosses over the water. I move towards it. Four giant eyebar chains hang between two redbrick towers. Each link of the red chain is a ten-foot iron bar. Against the dull sky, the imposing tower with its arched entry to the bridge is a gateway to Hell. Coming off the bridge, a group of teens chant about "King Billy" on a wall. The one at the front wields a Mars Bar, looping and rolling his arms like a conductor with a chocolate baton. The others bob and swing, bumping into each other and trying to get in my way.

'Millions come to see him,
they stand and gaze in awe,
they remember 1690,
King Billy's on the wall!'

The conductor thumps into me. After shoving the rest of the Mars Bar in his mouth, he mumbles around the obstruction: 'Watch where yer going, bud.' His group of cling-ons titter as they hurtle past.

Halfway over the suspension bridge, it's quiet. The Clyde ships are dark shadows floating in the mist, which is so thick that visibility is nil. I think about Daisy's new face, Greg forgetting my birthday, and about how school will be over soon. What else is going to change? What else is going to happen that has never happened before? Truth is, I'm jealous of them. They're both so sure of themselves. Sometimes, I've wished that I could change my face too, or at the very least grow a beard. Greg can grow a full beard in three weeks. If I don't shave for double that, all I'll have is patchy sideburns. I can't change, and there's nowhere to hide. Other thoughts and images try to push in, but I don't want them. I don't want to face that today.

The fog makes my skin wet, creeping in around me. The ends of the bridge become invisible from my spot in the middle.

'Away ye go, big man. Jump.' It's the Mars Bar muncher

who bumped into me earlier, the one conducting his football song. His buddies appear from the fog; they must've followed me. I count. Lucky number seven. Here are the famous Glasgow *neds*. All in white, as if they're sponsored by Adidas, Nike, and Reebok. Sovereign rings like knuckle-dusters on their fingers, gold chains bouncing about their necks as they jut their crew cuts in and out. They cluck and strut with nasal squawks. *Neds,* I conclude, are pigeons in tracksuits.

I'm surrounded. Adrenaline begins to pump.

'Are ye no listening, Paki? I said jump.' It's the ringleader, cawing through his nose. There's a golden hoop in his left ear, and one eyebrow has two lines shaved in.

'I'm thinking about it.' I attempt a smile, hoping a joke might get me out of this.

'O-ho! Fee-fi-fo-fum, I smell the blood of an Englishman. Here. How come this Paki sounds English? Should you no be speaking like "ooba gooba wah wah ching chong"?' He smirks at his mock Asian lingo.

'I'm Scottish, actually.'

'Yer kidding me on? Hear that boys, this Paki thinks he's Scottish.' The leader's fan club does a rehearsed schoolgirl-giggle.

'Look, piss off, the lot of you.' The more I try not to sound English, the more English my accent gets.

'Oooh, he's tough. Isn't he tough, Gerry?' That was the fat crony, rocking from foot to foot as if there are stones in his Air Max IIs.

'I don't want any trouble, Gerry. All I'm–'

'I donte wonte ehnee trouble Gerald,' he mocks in the queen's accent. Then he crowds me back against the bridge. 'Who're you calling Gerry, Paki?' The cronies chuckle, all elbows, nods and winks.

'He called you Gerry, Gerry.'

'Shut it,' to his crony, and then to me, 'think ye know me? Think we're pals?'

'No. I–'

'We're no pals, right? *You* don't get to call *me* Gerry. Right?'

'Sorry.'

'Awww, now he's sorry, eh?' He makes as if to punch me but stops at the last moment. I can't help it, I flinch, raising my arms to protect my head. They all laugh. Gerry turns left and right, making sure the group finds it as amusing as he does.

'Look at his face, Gerry. He's gonnae greet.'

'Aye, so he is. Ye gonnae greet, Paki? Have a wee piss in yer pants before we kick the shite out of ye? Is that it?'

I try to walk through them, but they tighten their semicircle, and Gerry shoves me back against the bridge. His lips coil into a smile.

I'm screwed.

'What do you want? Money?' I take out my wallet, showing the notes inside. I took a hundred quid with me and still have most of it.

'Aye, we'll take yer money,' he snatches my wallet and throws it over his shoulder without looking. One of the runts grabs it, takes out the notes and throws the wallet into the river. There goes my bank card. 'But money's no what we're after.' He puts his forehead against mine and pushes, daring me to look into his eyes. 'Ye get me?' A guy walks past the back of the group. In his fifties, head down, hands deep in his pockets. My eyes plea for acknowledgement. For help. But he knows what's going on; he fixes his gaze on the ground and walks faster. Gerry follows my line of sight to the man and smiles.

'What ye looking at him fer? He'll no help ye.' He clamps his forehead back against mine.

I doubt I would've stopped to help me either. A lump forms in my throat, but I won't allow tears to form in my eyes.

If they notice, it's all over. I'm supposed to be a black belt, and here are a group of kids toying with me. How come bullies always know who to pick on?

'Aw, we're kidding ye on. We're all pals here, big man. And we're no stupit enough tae fight some Paki on a bridge in the middle of the day, eh?' He extends his hand out towards me. And there I am again: ten years old and standing in front of Skud, but there's no Greg for protection this time. I know what's coming. He'll hit me, and it won't be a harmless kick on the arse. But what can I do? I place my hand into his.

He shakes it, then puts his arms into an I-give-up position.

'See bud,' he lifts his chin, 'we're all pals.'

I don't feel like pals, but I'm relieved. He moves to go, then turns back.

'Eh, got the time, big man?'

As soon as I look down at my watch, he punches me.

I jump right back up, try to break through their circle and run, but fat crony tackles me and holds my legs. The others kick at my ribs. Hands over my ears, I tuck into a foetus. But they pull my arms away so that Gerry can kick me in the face. We hadn't practised how to defend against this in karate. I don't feel pain. Not yet. Neurons fire too fast, adrenaline pumps round the system. Fight or flight. I squirm, struggling to keep my head out of the way of Gerry's foot, his Nike turning pink-red with blood. My eyes water and blur my vision. When he changes from kicks to stomps, I black out.

I come around, and it takes several seconds before I understand that it wasn't a nightmare. An old lady walks past without asking if I'm okay. I don't blame her, I must look like an alcoholic or a junkie. I drag myself to my feet, start the long walk towards the B&B. Footsteps echo behind me, but I don't dare turn around.

GREGOR: I doubt I need to explain it. You've surely figured it out by now. But for those who've missed it:

Video. Games. Are. All. I. Think. About.

It's hard to explain. Maybe you've an obsessive in your family? An uncle that loves football more than he loves his wife? A granny that's so nuts for Tom Jones she remortgaged her house to go to every show on his last world tour? Being obsessive is learned behaviour.

My dad's mental about Country and Western music. Started teaching my brothers guitar when they were three. Forced them to sing Kenny Rogers and John Denver at family parties. Luckily, my brothers liked it. My younger brother, Kev, went to Nashville to record his own album (nobody bought it, but at least he tried). Dad did the guitar thing with me too. But I didn't get it. What I did get was the *behaviour* of obsession. Where Dad's office is full of cowboy memorabilia, my room's a shrine to video games.

Nobody cares about it when you're young. It's a quirk. There's nothing to do in the North East of Scotland, so gaming's one way to pass the time. But not for me. When Daize and I got together, she'd no idea that my "wee obsession" was already all-consuming. I know I'm expected to "grow up", but at this point, I can't imagine a brain-free second when I *won't* think about video games. As I get older, my obsession's starting to take on a different meaning for me and my relationship with Daisy.

Case in point: Daisy's forever asking me, 'What are you thinking?' I get asked this at least twice a day. But lately, I don't tell the truth. We'll be walking Lumpy, sharing a burger, or lying in bed, and I can't tell her that I'm thinking about video games. Sometimes, the game's paused on the TV screen in the corner of the room, waiting for me to get back to it. These days, I say things like 'I'm thinking about Australia' which isn't what I'm thinking about at all. It's what Daisy wants to hear.

Video games are my life. I don't give a crap how stupid that sounds. They're my go-to buddy when I'm happy, sad, angry, or tired. I don't know how to make a non-obsessive understand that. I know Daisy thinks the *Street Fighter II* trophy is a silly bit of plastic. But that trophy means for me what my dad's guitar means for him. It's a symbol. Like my brothers going to America just to buy cowboy boots. Like the box of Nashville albums in Kev's garage. Country music is part of them, and my trophies are part of me.

The first time I won this competition, it was a dozen of us standing around a boxed arcade game. But each year, more and more come to try and dethrone me. Last year, when we switched to the Super Nintendo over the arcade version, there was a record thirty-six competitors. I'm the best at something, and it's a good feeling to be the best at something. It's hard to explain that without sounding smug, but it's true. It might not be something important, or fashionable, or that pays a lot of money. But when I play this game, I'm more than a schoolkid who works part-time in a crappy supermarket. This trophy is more than a bit of plastic. It's part of my identity.

And in a few months, exams are going to be over, school finished forever. And everything feels like it's slipping away. Ever since Daisy's operation, it's been like a time-bomb counting down. I'm trying to hold us together. And I need this. I need it more than ever. Because maybe she saw my bank book and discovered my secret. But I know her secret too. I figured it out at her house last night when she slipped up and forgot to cover her tracks. I saw. And she's been lying to me for months.

DAISY: J's wounds look worse than they are. His puffy jaw's gone down with the ice, and the black eyes are 'cause of his broken nose. He reckons there's no real reason to go to a hospital. Once again, the pair of them're bickering about the karate suits.

'I'm Ken,' says J.

'You're Ryu,' says Greg. J getting his head kicked in has switched Greg into protective mode. 'Look, I was a total dickbag earlier. That stuff in the lavvy. I didn't–I'm sorry. It doesn't matter what I wear, I use my hands to play the game, and we're here for your birthday, remember?' It's hard not to find him cute when he's like this. I felt like such a bitch when Greg told me what happened earlier. And I can't believe we forgot J's eighteenth. We've been way too embroiled in our own crap.

I'm still mad at Greg for blowing the Australia money and being a dick. But his shame at missing J's birthday, his protectiveness over him, they remind me of his good qualities. Blood all over your best friend's face will do that. It gives you perspective on pointless arguments.

Greg puts a hand on J's shoulder:

'You got the crap kicked out of you. So, you're like the real Ryu, a wandering warrior who battles the scum of the Earth.'

'Don't make this romantic, Greg, I'm still pissed at you two for not phoning the police.'

'We spoke about it, Daize. The neds'll be long gone by now, and J's cancelled his bank card; nobody needs the police here.'

'Still. Those wee idiots can't think they can go around doing this to people.'

'I'm fine,' J says to nobody, and then to me, 'I'm fine.'

He's far from fine. The wounds are one thing, but he came back to the B&B and was silent for ages. It took us an hour to get the story out of him. I think he was more upset that we forgot his birthday than anything else. Now he's adamant that he's coming to the final and that this isn't going to spoil his weekend.

'We didn't come here to fight, so let's stop fighting. We came here for Greg to win that money. Then we can go to Australia and swim with sharks and hug koala bears and shag kangaroos. I'm going to watch Greg win his trophy, and I don't care if anyone's waiting in the shadows to try and stop me. That's what we bloody well came here for, and that's what I'm bloody well doing.'

'Also,' adds Greg, 'you'll be the most authentic looking Ryu in Glasgow.'

I wink and throw the red gi at him.

'Shut your face and put it on.'

JUNAID: I can't remember the last time I tied a karate belt around my waist. Still, my fingers tuck and tighten as if it were yesterday. What a fraud. My hands are still shaking a little, but nobody has noticed. The fight on the bridge has brought all kinds of thoughts to the front of my mind.

Daisy inspects us as we stand in our gis. I'm a little under six feet, which is a full six inches taller than Greg, but the heel on his John Wayne footwear gives him a boost. I'm no muscle-bound action hero, but I don't look out of place in my gi, either. After all, I used to wear the thing all the time. Greg's stocky frame fills his gi out in a different way, his thick legs and shoulders making it tight in places. His grungy ginger hair, grizzly beard and cowboy boots actually suit him. And gis have a way of making people look cool.

'You guys look magic.' Daisy disappears into the bathroom. Greg ties his headband tight as if he's Rambo's bastard love child.

'Thanks, babe.' With Daize out of the room, it's as if he's said it to me. Then he says: 'Let's do this.' The incident in the toilet earlier is already forgotten. In fact, everyone's getting on a lot better since I got beat up.

When she comes out of the bathroom, Daisy's dressed as Chun-Li, the only female character in *Street Fighter*. Her hair is in white buns, her eyes have long lashes and blue make-up. She even has the white boots and spiked bracelets. Daisy is the same height as Greg, but the cut of the dress and four-inch heel on her boots make her almost as tall as me. The silky blue dress comes a little above the knee front and back but is slit right to the top of her thighs at the sides. We did *not* know she would be dressed like this.

'Sweet Holy Jesus!' Greg hops off the bed for a closer look. 'You look. I mean. Whoa!'

She stands there with her feet wide and winks, a finger on her smiling pink mouth. Her other hand makes a "peace sign" above her head; the pose Chun-Li does in the game after winning a fight. I smile.

'You look brilliant, Daize,' Greg adds:

'This is awesome, Daize. You can get in front of the other guys at the tournament and distract them!' Greg and Daisy embrace and whisper sorrys and sweet nothings that I can't make out. There goes the jealousy again, despite the refound love for my friends. A short, sharp burst of crocodile mutilation. I suppress as much as I can and try to enjoy everyone being back to normal.

GREGOR: The competitors are between thirteen and thirty years old. About half of them are dressed as characters from the game. As usual, there're more Ryus than Kens. Among the other players I see:

1/. Four guys in army fatigues and spiked hair (Guile).

2/. A couple of guys in red suits and capes (M. Bison–the final boss in the game).

3/. A thick-set bloke who's cut his hair and grown a Russian Wrestler beard (Zangief).

And:

4/. A dark-skinned guy with mystic yogi face paint (Dhalsim).

The TVs blare with the tunes of the different stages, volumes jacked up to exploding. I notice three or four Chun-Lis, but my Chun-Li is by far the most authentic in the room. Then I see one of the other Ryus from the afternoon, a twelve-year-old called Albert. Wee rascal's made it to the finals and is the only person I haven't played in previous years. I start to relax. It's going to be okay. I close my eyes, visualise the smile on Daisy's face as I'm handed the cheque.

J gives me a nudge.

'Look, Greg. Dominik Diamond is here.'

So, the rumours were true. Dominik's the presenter of *GamesMaster*, the only programme about video games on TV. He moseys onto the stage in his John Lennon glasses, suit and cravat. I've always wanted to be on the show; I've applied a few times but never got a response. With Dominik here, the competitive atmosphere amplifies (unfortunately, without the TV cameras). It's another pressure, but another big reason to win the comp again–if I win, Dominik might put in a good word and get me a spot on the show. Daisy suffers through *GamesMaster* episodes because she knows I love them, but still, she says:

'If you win a *GamesMaster* golden joystick, it's mine.'

She knows fine well if I ever win a *GamesMaster* golden joystick, it's going on top of my lavvy.

'Ladies and Gamer-men. I'm Dominik Diamond, and I'm grumpy. But don't worry, I'll have cheered up later in the year when I'll be back on your screens on *GamesMaster*.'

A quick mini-chant of 'Games-Mas-ter! Games-Mas-ter!' circulates the room.

'Forget about that tonight, though. Forget about your joysticks, golden or otherwise, and concentrate on the challenge ahead. Tonight, eight contestants, some physically attractive, others laughably ugly, will fight to the death. Welcome one. Welcome, all. To the annual. Scottish. *Street Fighter II*. Championshiiiiips!'

Relaxation disappears. My belly does a backflip.

JUNAID: This one time, when we were kids, Greg's mum took us to Laser Quest in Aberdeen. A warehousey building with arcade machines, bowling lanes, and a state-of-the-art laser tag setup. We'd been before and were equally matched. It must have been early or late or a weeknight or something, because we got to play laser tag on our own. The fantastical inside had fake rocks and walls, mirrorballs and hidey holes. It was me versus Greg, one on one.

When we went in, Greg ran behind the first rock on the left, and I ran to one on the opposite side. The "rock" was made of wood and paper. The laser tag area was dark but for blobs of red light that lava lamped up and down the walls to create the effect that we were on Mars. Atmospheric music from war films pumped through the speakers. Smoke machines went "HSSSST!" And us clipped inside American footballish armour, with "laser" guns that didn't shoot *Star Trek* beams. We each ran five feet from the door, and there we stayed, firing back and forth from behind the safety of papier-mâché rocks.

I wanted to zoom out and into the broader world of the Laser Quest warehouse. I wanted to move in a HSSSST! of smoke without Greg spotting me, so I could find a better vantage point, attack him from behind. We both wanted to win as much as the other. Which is why we wasted his mum's money by not moving, standing and shooting, point for point, kill for kill, behind those rocks the whole time.

While we took off the sensor-armour in the locker room, a guy printed off little receipts with the data of the game. It was a draw. We'd killed each other twenty-seven times. I don't know why I remember that, but it was twenty-seven hits each. A kill pretty much each minute, every minute, five feet from the entrance. Neither wanted to risk running out from his safe spot, afraid that it might cost him everything.

DAISY: There's a friendly atmosphere in the pub. Sure it's nerdy. We're all dressed up as computer game characters. And the geeky guy from that snoozefest TV programme gets his name chanted. But it's sweet. I'd rather be here than at a football match in the pissing rain any day of the week. It's safe, like a family reunion. J and I have polished off two pitchers of "Taxi Driver" and are halfway through a pitcher of "The Shining". The booze lubricates our chants during Greg's matches.

The quarters go by with the help of another pitcher, and Dominik has a couple of the losers onstage for comments.

'What can I say, guys? It wasn't meant to be tonight. The competition was too tough. Anjelica, the last remaining girl in our championship this evening, have you got any advice for our semi-finalists?'

'Well Dominik, as I often say to my boyfriend, keep those fingers moving.'

'Keep those fingers moving indeed. Grant, who's Anjelica's boyfriend I'm told?' Grant nods. 'How do you feel about your girlfriend's advice to the boys?'

'She's got a point Dominik, but the wrist is just as important.'

'We've got some right cheeky beggars in the Dungeon tonight. However, they'll have to take their fingers and wrists home *without* the *Scottish Street Fighter II Championship* trophy. But to ease the shame and burden of your beatings, here are your tokens for free drinks and onion rings. Everybody, a round of applause for our quarter-finalists.'

Greg moves into the semis to face a guy who plays (but definitely isn't dressed as) Chun-Li. A twelve-year-old called

Albert and a guy dressed as a soldier are the other semi-finalists.

Greg destroys Chun-Li 20 fights to 11.

'Greg! On top form, and our first finalist of the year. Your fourth final in a row, and, I'm told, your victory here is a record for a semi-final, winning by nine clear matches. Tell me, how does it feel to be in the final again?'

'It feels great, Dominik. This is my championship, I've trained hard, and I'm not going home without my trophy. I've got a space ready for it on my shelf next to the other three.'

It's close now, and I'm relieved. Greg'll either have to win against either a twelve-year-old whose bedtime must've been hours ago or the soldier. And I'm sure he beat the soldier guy last year. How hard could it be?

GREGOR: Albert-the-twelve-year-old-Ryu destroys Danny, who plays the character Guile, 20-4. This is upsetting for two reasons. First, because my record win for a semi-final's already broken. And second, because I beat Danny in the final two years ago as well as the quarters last year. I've got Danny sussed, but I've never played Albert before. He's good.

Dominik has him on the stage. 'So, Albert. Greg sets a record, and you immediately beat it! Sixteen matches the difference between you and your opponent. How do you feel about getting through to the final to play against another Ryu?'

'I'll smash him,' says Albert, punching one hand into the other.

'Smashing. And is that your dad over there? How does he like you playing *Street Fighter* all the time?'

'He plays with me, but I smash him too.'

'There you have it, a family of smashers. Now, Danny, you didn't win many rounds there, what were the special tactics that made Albert so difficult to beat?'

'He's too fast, Dominik. I also practised all afternoon and think that I tired my hand out.'

'Hand fatigue. The death of many a good man. Here's your token, go grab yourself a drink and some onion rings. Everybody, we'll take a twenty-minute break so that Albert can rest before the final.'

During the break, I look at Daisy gibbering with J and think about our time together. What'll happen if she goes to Australia without me? Until the argument this week, I'd never thought about it. It was all so far away–the end of school and the holiday in Australia. At least, they both felt far away a couple of weeks ago, but now everything's moving so fast.

This. Us. Sitting in pubs playing video games and getting dressed up. I hoped it would all carry on when we went to university. Business as usual. But it's blatantly not part of Daisy's Master Plan. Not unless I can convince her otherwise.

Dominik calls me and Albert up for the last match of the evening. I settle into my chair. This is it. This is my moment to hold everything together. Winning this money and the trip in the summer could help to change her mind. Albert turns his head to give Daisy (and her outfit) twelve-year-old sex-eyes. He licks his lips as he drinks her in. Then the cocky little dickbag looks at me, smiles, and winks.

TRACK 5: SECRETS

JUNAID: It's kind of a secret, but I kissed Daisy before Greg knew she existed. It was the third week of the summer holidays. One of those days when walking barefoot burnt the soles of your feet. A day which made your fingertips tingle with anticipation.

There was a group of tents set up at a section of beach known as the "Campull". A grassy area opened up to the white-sand shoreline, where picture-postcard dunes stretched the eleven miles to the next town along the coast. The tents were set back from the sand, pitched at the foot of a slope with a WWII pillbox on top. There were nine tents in all. On closer inspection, I noticed that apart from two women, the campers were all girls. Pretty girls, with rolled-up shorts and t-shirts which clung to their sticky backs.

Word got around fast. Within an hour, every local lad had congregated in the field above the campsite. Bubblegum pop poured from a stereo. The girls ate burgers on sesame seed buns and sausages on sticks from a barbeque. They sucked ketchup from their fingers, oil dribbling down sun-kissed chins. We used the old pillbox as a lookout down to the tents. I approached Bob, a kid from my class, cool as a crunchy cucumber.

'Has anyone figured out what's with all the babes?'

'They're Guides.'

'Girl Guides?'

'No, Man Guides.'

'Cool.'

'Here's what's cool. That one wants to meet up after the guide leaders are sleeping.' Bob pointed to a blonde-haired, pixie-eared Guide in tiny green shorts. Aileen Hendry. A prized babe from school. Word on the grapevine was that she'd split up from her boyfriend, a respected footballer in fourth year. They'd been together for two and a half months, which at that point in life counted as a long-term relationship.

'Aileen Hendry wants to meet up?'

'Yup. Asked us if we could get booze and if we knew what to do with a block of hash.'

'Hash?'

'This is once-in-a-lifetime stuff, Pinglish. Sarah Donald is down there.' I didn't fight over my "nickname" these days. I still hated it, but I was used to it. I was more concerned with the other name used, an infamous girl from the year above:

'Blowjob Donald?'

'The one and only. And hands off. She's mine.'

I looked at the sun high in the afternoon sky and sneezed. When I blinked, golden rings hung in the air. The sky was blue and empty, a blank canvas on which to paint the future. The Guides had brought out a sense of brotherhood and teamwork. We went around our houses to collect all the stuff we'd need. Sleeping bags, pillows, snacks. We swiped booze from homes that wouldn't notice if a bottle or two went missing. We collected my trusty tent, and then we waited.

Beezer said we'd all get laid that night if we "played our cards right". As a rule, we laughed or made fun when Beezer and his wobbly belly said stuff about girls. But no one laughed today. We knew he was onto something. We felt through the soles of our hot feet on the pillbox roof that this would be a game changer. A rite of passage all boys go through on the way to manhood. We spoke about getting "rubber johnnies", everyone acting as if they'd used them. I knew all that anyone had done with condoms was have a "posh wank". But girls our age definitely had sex; we could list a few who'd left school to have kids before they were sixteen. Some of the guys claimed to have squeezed boobs. Others to have slipped a hand up a skirt at school discos to pinch an arse. But this was different. This was Blowjob Donald.

Anything was possible.

Lisa was the girl I'd set my sights on. She was a little taller than I was, and her hair fell in loops halfway down her back. Her legs were long and brown, and her smile had a cute gap between her front teeth. She'd laughed at the jokes I wrote on bits of cardboard torn from their burger packets. Kissing Lisa was all I thought about for the rest of the day. How I'd put my hands on her hips, and what I'd do with my lips and tongue. In a private moment when I'd sloped off to pee in the dunes, I practised on my hand.

At 2 AM on the nose, Aileen Hendry and Sarah Donald were fumbling with the zips on my tent door. Lisa came in first, flanked by a couple of girls I didn't recognise from the afternoon. All the boys were there, too: me, Steve, Bob, Beezer and Euan. Greg was on a Disney holiday in Florida with his parents, his brothers tagging along to buy cowboy boots. He would be gutted that he missed out on this. But the numbers were five on five like it was meant to be. Us boys had drunk a bit of cider and played cards to stay awake, but the girls were a different beast. They had been hammering wine for an hour in their own tents and were well on their way to oblivion. Especially Lisa, who had a red face, and whose head hung at the neck.

'Is she okay?'

'Ach, she's fine,' said Sarah Donald, 'aren't you Lise?' Lisa raised her head and smiled, which seemed to take a lot of effort. 'See?' A plastic bottle of cider came my way. I took an optimistic swig. This could still be the night, I thought. But with that, there was a high-pitched voice outside the tent:

'Girls! Get out of there right now!'

We went silent, there was nowhere to hide.

'Aw, shite,' said Aileen, 'we're dead.'

Then the zip began to open, but it wasn't a Guide leader who popped their head into the tent–it was Skud. The girls laughed, and the boys slapped his back and invited him in, passing him the cider. He took a massive gulp.

'What are we playing?'

'Spin the bottle?' suggested Sarah.

'Aye,' went Aileen Hendry, finishing off a bottle of wine. 'Me first.'

The bottle stopped on Steve, and we agreed that the snogging should last fifteen seconds. Aileen seemed chuffed, Steve like the cat who got the cream. They pressed their tongues into each others' mouths as we counted down, slapping our hands on our thighs.

Skud volunteered to go next.

'Fifteen seconds is nothing, let's make it *thirty*.' When the bottle stopped on Lisa, I deflated. She'd long forgotten the notes we'd passed that day, knee-walking into the middle of the tent to do the duty. She closed her eyes and parted her lips. Skud slithered into the circle, leaning into her without hesitation. They began to kiss, Lisa with her arms around his neck, everyone counting down but me. Skud pushed his hands up into her hoody, the boys wriggling to get a closer look. I saw the knuckles of Lisa's spine, the strap of her bra. The tent cheered as it continued the count, slowing down to make the dare last longer.

'Sixteen, fifteen, fourteen…' It seemed to last forever, their mouths opening and closing like goldfish. Skud was unable to keep from grinning, his tongue hanging out. As Lisa licked and bit at it, Skud found my eyes across the tent. I hated him for doing that, for rubbing my face in it.

Afterwards, Lisa moved back to her seat, readjusting her top. Then it was my turn. As you might have guessed, the bottle stopped on one of the girls I didn't know. The one with the chin. This was, of course, thirteen-year-old Daisy, years away from braces and facial reconstruction. I put my mouth on hers. I was determined to keep it closed, but the rest of them jeered until I opened up. Daisy put her tongue in, flicking it about until I pulled away.

'That wasn't a snog!'

'It wasn't thirty seconds either!'

I screwed up my face in disgust.

'It's not my fault, her breath stinks!' Everyone cracked up, and I felt bad about saying that, but I needed a reason for not kissing her properly. Skud had thrown me off. It was all wrong, kissing in front of each other like some kind of spectacle. Before we could be forced to go again, Beezer pointed at her:

'She's going to whitey!'

He opened the tent door, and the girls shoved her out into the night. Daisy managed a few steps, then threw up the afternoon's BBQ over the side of the pillbox. Skud was quick on the draw:

'Jesus, Pinglish, you must be one *terrible* kisser!' Then everyone was laughing at me.

I avoided Daisy's eye when we crossed paths at school, looked the other way in the playground and the corridors. I hoped that she'd been so drunk she couldn't remember anything about that night. But after I thought it was all behind me, she got together with Greg. She didn't say anything for weeks. But after we knew each other a little better, Daisy offered me a breath mint with a look in her eye. We both burst out laughing. It might seem ridiculous, but it's something we have that even Greg doesn't know about.

GREGOR: The final is epic. First to 30 wins.

We're allowed to fight as the same character. There's a cheat that lets the pair of us choose Ryu, and wee Albert wants it bad. I lose the first five bouts. But I soon click on to his tactics and come back with eight straight wins for a three-match lead. There's no ventilation in the Dungeon, and cigarette smoke clings to the low ceiling. I use drops to moisten my eyes between rounds and don't care who's watching. The noise of the pub, the game, and Dominik's commentary blur together. I'm focussed, it's like the sounds are in a different room.

At the halfway mark, Albert's won 16 matches to my 14. Dominik calls a break, and I go to Daize and J, who are on the sofa closest to the action. J leaves to get me a Red Bull, Daisy rubs my shoulders, and I close my eyes and breathe. I need to keep my focus on the Master Plan; I intend on sticking to it. I'm doing this for Daisy. For us. Her mam's better than I've ever seen her and Daize is officially part of my family. My mam and dad love her, my brothers treat her like a little sister. I can't lose her now.

After the break, the rounds pass more or less on an even keel. I manage to get things back on track at twenty-seven all, but not for long.

'And another flying uppercut from Albert sends Greg crashing to the concrete. It's match for match here as we're approaching thirty for both players. Greg twenty-seven, Albert twenty-eight.'

Match fifty-six goes to Albert.

'Bollocks!' I say to nobody, raising my controller. I restrain myself from throwing it across the room at the last second.

'Zen master Greg might finally be losing his cool as Albert moves one match from taking the title.'

Albert hasn't won yet. This is *my* championship.

I look back at Daisy, who seems worried. Does she sense a loss coming? No. I can do this. I can come back from this.

Match fifty-seven: Mine.

Match fifty-eight: Mine.

'Holy Hadouken fireballs, ladies and gents, he's done it, he's brought it back to twenty-nine all. The 1994 *Scottish Street Fighter II Championship* trophy has come down to the *final match*! What a night. Boys, does anyone need a break before the last fight?'

We shake our heads and take long slugs of Red Bull. I put drops in my tired eyes. Albert's dad dries his son's hands with a towel while Albert cricks his neck left and right.

I close my eyes and visualise what I need to do. I need to win this next match. To collect the cheque and my fourth trophy. That's how I'll keep her. Make everything okay again. And at that point, when I've proved myself on this stage in front of everyone, I'll get down on one knee and ask Daisy Parker to be my wife.

DAISY: We'd set up our tents at a bit of Cairn Bay beach called the "Campull". Don't ask me how these places get their names. The stretches of beach around here all have funny nicknames: the Campull, New Shore, Bally's Lum, The Cut. We were camped below a pillbox, listening to cheddar pop tunes, playing games we were already too old for. But we knew adventure would find us.

It came in the form of boys.

A motley crew of patchwork toerags popped their heads

out from behind the pillbox. The Cairn Bay *loons* (local speak for "boys") were a jumble of pasty legs and tanned arms. Our Guide leaders mumbled under their breath about keeping the boys away from their innocent girls. Ironic, seeing as half of us'd already smoked pilfered fags at a nearby dip in the sand dunes. Aileen Hendry had told the boys that she had some "skunk".

'I bet the boys pretend to get stoned off it,' she said. It wasn't drugs; it was oregano from her mum's spice rack. 'Look at them. Heads sticking out above the grass, trying to hide their hard-ons!' Aileen relished the word, squealing as she said it.

'I'll take care of their hard-ons,' said Sarah Donald, moving her hand next to her face and poking her tongue into her cheek. We cackled at her filthiness. Sarah was the oldest and allegedly gave out unceremonious blowjobs to boys at the far end of Invergowan graveyard. Especially to the boyfriends of "lassies too scared to touch a willy". Half the prudes at school were out for Sarah's blood. It was all a load of rubbish, but I still looked at her with a kind of awe; she seemed so grown up.

Away from our mams and dads, in a cut in the dunes, we felt a kind of freedom; we could be who we wanted. The afternoon went like that until Bob Elric gave Sarah a note that said: "Geez a BJ Sarah". Her reputation had preceded her. I later caught the pair of them in a sand dune. Pants and knickers round their knees, Bob's milky fourteen-year-old arse bouncing enthusiastically above Sarah's hearty frame. She left school a year later when the baby was born, and they're expecting another. Bob's an apprentice mechanic now. I gained a kind of respect for both of them that day. Not 'cause of their underage shenanigans, more cause of an attitude they had. Something I was endeavouring to develop.

Don't get me wrong, there was no chance I was letting Bob or anybody else put their hard-ons anywhere near me. But I was more than ready for my first kiss, lagging behind everyone else at school.

Enter Junaid Jarvis.

Junaid Jarvis was a teenage dream. Huge brown eyes and a broad smile, as well as an innocence lacking in his horny, testosterone-fuelled pals. He was a dishy, mixed-race, boy-next-door type, even if he didn't dress like it. He wore trainers with no socks, tight shorts and a t-shirt that said "Be Like Water" with a picture of Bruce Lee on the front. But who cared about clothes when someone had skin and an accent like that? We were all pasty white and desperate to tan. The more ginger among us hid from UV rays and used factor fifty sun cream. J's skin was the perfect colour all year round. His parents had also forced him to adopt their Kentish accent. He sounded so exotic. It was love at first listen when I heard him in the school corridors, and I'd dreamt about this camping trip since it was first mentioned at Guides. If he wanted to put his tongue in my mouth, I wasn't going to stop him.

The boys and girls arranged a rendezvous for the middle of the night. I was out by 1 AM, listening to waves calling out at the stars. It was then I came across Sarah and Bob, the moon like a sun and shining bright on Bob's arse.

'Wrap yer legs round,' he said, 'it keeps falling out.'

When we met in the boys' tent, it was 2 AM. My quiet "hello" lacked confidence, and I took to the booze for a bit of Dutch courage. That sounds like we were alcoholics, but there was only a bottle of wine and a litre of cheap cider between more than a dozen of us.

This guy Skud turned up. Lisa took a shine to him, which was good for me, cause J obviously fancied her. I tried to get drunk fast. The drunker I got, the easier it'd be.

Aileen snogged Steve, a blonde-haired, blue-eyed footballer for the village under 16s. They licked and lapped as everybody watched on, getting excited about their turn. Some other couples paired off before it was J's turn to spin the bottle. Fate was on my side, and it stopped at me. Struggling to keep the smile off my face, I bit my lips from the inside. I was determined to hide my pre-straightened teeth, which I hated even more than my underbite.

I moved out into the middle of the tent; my time had come. J made a big show of coming close, taking forever. I had to lean in first. I puckered my lips, hoping that he knew enough to lead me through the magical moment that was about to occur. Instead, he closed his eyes and screwed up his face in disgust. Our lips touched, but he never opened his mouth. None of the tongues or wetness or hot breath you find in sexy novels. Just lips, like in a black and white film. I tried to put my tongue in, but J locked his mouth shut then pulled away.

'Your breath stinks.' My hand covered my mouth. Did my breath smell? I wanted to cry as the whole tent laughed, but was also determined not to leave.

And that was my first kiss. If you could call it a kiss at all.

After us, Skud and Lisa went to town on a thirty-second kiss which was more like what I'd imagined for myself. Lisa spewed soon afterwards and had to go to bed. Then there was this weird interaction between Skud and J. J half-whispered something which provoked Skud:

'You speaking to me, Pinglish?'

'I never said anything,' replied J.

'I'd keep it that way if I were you.'

The exchange had me confused, but it shut J up. He went home not long after that, in the middle of the night, fuming. Scaredy J.

Skud rolled a joint with the "skunk" and taught us how we should inhale "if we wanted to feel anything". Us girls couldn't stop laughing as the boys acted tough passing round the oregano joint. We moved on to truth or dare. Everybody spilt the beans about how far they'd gone. For most of us in the tent, that night had been our first kiss. Aileen confessed that she'd let her ex put a hand up her bra in a pile of hay at a barn dance. They'd broken up because she wouldn't go further. Sarah slapped Bob's thigh, telling everyone that they'd already shagged that very night. We all laughed and cheered as Bob's face went beetroot. The comment about my breath was already forgotten. When I said that I'd never even snogged anybody, Skud jumped in.

'Right, count us down.'

He kissed me properly, tongue and all. I felt so grown up, I'd wanted to get my first kiss over with that night and had managed to do it. And you know what? Everybody's breath smelt the same–like smoke and pickled onion Monster Munch and cheap wine. The boys dared Sarah and Aileen to snog, but they couldn't do it for laughing. Still, they gave each other a peck on the lips that the boys would remember forever. Bob and Sarah wanted to shag without Sarah "getting sand up her crack," so we left them alone in the tent to make their first baby. The rest of us took the sleeping bags and went over the dunes to watch the sun come up. As the sun sparkled on the water, I felt different. I'd kissed a boy and had a few sips of wine. I was ten times cooler than I'd been at the start of the day.

So, no, my first real kiss wasn't J the prude. It was Skud. A perfect gentleman who didn't say anything about my chin, my teeth or my breath. When J and I became friends, I offered him a mint one day, to see what he would do. He blushed and squirmed, but then we laughed. Peace-offering. Truce. It's become like a secret handshake between us, one that even Greg doesn't know. Well, here's another secret, just between you and me:

Skud was a *much* better kisser than Junaid Jarvis.

TRACK 6: PLAY FOR TODAY

JUNAID: Daisy comes back from the nightclub toilets with smeared make up. We do a couple of tequila shots and she drags me to the dancefloor. The booze picks us up from our dip at the end of the competition.

We discarded Greg (and our costumes) at the B&B, and now the night is about us. I'm wide awake. We throw shapes like cockatoos. I've no idea what I'm doing with my hands and legs, but Daisy doesn't notice or doesn't care. She bites my hand, and I scream. Boys approach, shouting in her ear, but she shakes her head, points at me and keeps punching her fists in the air. We spin, drop low and bounce high. The house music thump, thump, thumps. Each song puts Greg further and further away. Each brings Daisy closer and closer.

We sweat and drink water and sweat some more. Our clammy fingers intertwine. Her hair stuck to her forehead, she turns and grinds backwards into me, looking up to give a wicked smile. Snapping back around, her eyes stare hard into mine. She's pissed off. Excited. I pull her in close, her hot breath in my ear.

'Let's get out of here,' she says.

Greg isn't a blip on my mind.

DAISY: I wash my face at the sink and then lock myself in a cubicle. A dingy nightclub on a dingy street in a dingy city. I don't even need to pee. I need a break. I need to get away from here. Away from Greg. I cry but don't bother hiding my sobs cause the music's so loud.

I couldn't believe he went snooping in my stuff. I couldn't believe he said what he said.

I'm so angry that I want to fight, to hit somebody. Then he passed out, oblivious. I want something to happen. I want to fall in love with somebody else. To dance, to move, to do something stupid, make him as angry as I am. I want to forget about video games and Australia. About anything beyond the next song, the next drink, the next–

'You all right in there?' Says a head from above my cubicle.

'Fine,' I say, but can't hide the wobble in my voice. Then I cry on a stranger's shoulder for fifteen minutes before washing my face, and deciding that for the rest of the night, Gregor Buchan does not exist.

JUNAID: Greg lost the deciding fight of the tournament in a match that lasted seventeen seconds. So we didn't worry too much when he drank a whole pitcher of "The Shining" through a straw. He'd a right to drown his sorrows, after all. But then Greg had a second, and a third pitcher. Not long after he'd left us to get his fourth of the evening, we heard a scream from the bar.

'It's *my* trophy! I worked all year for that, you dickbags!' We shot off our seats and bundled up the stairway.

'You need to calm down, mate. You've had your fun.' The barman, dishtowel over his shoulder, had his fists halfway to a boxing guard. He was more than ready to pounce on our drunken Musketeer. Greg had a pitcher in each hand. An empty above his head, which he threatened to hurl at anyone who approached, and a full one at his mouth. He sucked on the straws so hard that his eyes bulged from their sockets like a comic book villain.

After finishing the fourth pitcher, he held the jug above his head in the same manner. Daisy and I had weaved our way to the front of the ruckus, Greg's head flopping on his shoulders. The barman plotted his move, recruiting his staff to help him.

'I'll grab him. You boys get those bloody jugs before he lobs them.' But Daisy was in the line of fire before anyone.

'Greg. Put the pitchers down.' Her voice shocked Greg's neck-bobbing head back to a neutral position.

'Daize?' He struggled to locate his girlfriend, a life-size character from his favourite video game, standing right in front of him. 'Is…Daize?' This is what happens when you down four pitchers of "The Shining" after weeks off the booze. Daisy smiled and opened her arms. Greg embraced her like a crab, his giant glass pincers gave an overlapping clunk.

'I lost, Daize. Four in a row.'

I eased the jugs from his grasp and placed them on the bar. The barman whipped the towel from his shoulder.

'Get him out.'

Greg whimpered and shuddered in Daisy's arms, which could only mean one thing. He pushed Daisy back, bent at the waist, convulsing. Without looking up, he stretched his arms out in a give-me-space gesture. All four pitchers exited his body. A brown mess chunked with onion rings, coming back the way it went down. Most of it landed on the lower half of his gi. *My* gi.

'Get him out. Now! And he's barred. Don't bother coming back.'

I put my mouth onto Daisy's and my hands into her damp hair. My heart pounds to the beat of the techno music.

Around the back of the nightclub, we can still hear the thump, thump, thump of the tunes inside. My brain is alert, racing. Daisy's hands move over my clothes, and it's all happening. Everything. I've thought about this moment but never expected it to happen. My jacket's off my shoulders, and she puts it on the ground.

'Lie down.'

DAISY: Outside the pub, J and I each took a side of Greg. We hooked our arms under his and walked him through the maze of traffic lights at Charing Cross. He zig-zagged us left and right as his weight sloshed around inside him. He stopped to throw up every couple of minutes, but without wretching. He's been in this state before. His silent, pukey tap state.

'Get a change of clothes for him will you, J? We'll never get him in the B&B like this.'

We changed Greg out of his sodden costume in a laundromat doorway on the next street over. I buttoned and tucked and zipped him up while J went to throw the karate suit into a bin across the road.

'That was the gi I wore when I got my black belt. Looks more like a filled nappy now.'

'Sorry, J.'

'It's not your fault.'

Greg looked passably human. J looked around.

'We should get some food in him. There's got to be a chip shop down on the main street.'

'Can you manage something to eat, Greg? A bag of chips?'

Greg gabbled nonsense, punctuated with "sorrys" and "love yous". Coming out of his drunk, pukey mouth, those words had never been so empty. We put him on the pavement outside the *Three-in-One* chipper. I stayed to hold him up while J went in for fish and chips. I looked at Gregor Buchan. At myself. At the state of us.

I shook him.

'I've had enough, Greg. I want out. I'm sick and tired of waiting around for something to happen. There's more to life than eating chips on street corners in Glasgow, dressed up like computer games.'

'Video games,' he grumbled.

'We need to go. *GREG*? I need to get out of here.'

'What?' His head was between his knees.

'Do you hear me? We need to go.'

'Go where?' He rolled his head to the side to look at me.

'Australia. Tomorrow.'

'We're not going to Australia tomorrow, Daize. Get a grip.' His head rolled back.

'Okay, maybe not *go* tomorrow, but we could *book it,* couldn't we? We could book it, so we know that it's real.'

'Grow up, Daisy. We're not going to Australia. We were never really going. Just like you were never going to come to uni with us.' I flinched. He didn't lift his head up to say it, kept it down between his knees. Then he passed out, falling sideways onto the pavement. I needed a minute to take all that in. What it meant.

Greg must've been looking through my stuff. That was going to be a hard conversation. But other things became clear then too. He'd never had any intention of going to Australia either. He doesn't give a crap about what I want. Drunken nights at video game competitions and moving into a house across the street from his mam. That's the extent of the Greg Buchan "Master Plan". When did he ever ask for my input? It's all about him, and I'm expected to go along with everything.

One of Sylvia's black figs drops off the tree. More accurately, I pull the little bastard off and launch it into next week.

JUNAID: Afterwards, we laughed. We were on my jacket by the bins behind the nightclub.

Ridiculous.

With no desire to go back to the B&B, we decide to walk off the booze. We can't stop walking. We walk and talk for what could be hours. I take Daize to the bridge where I got beat up, show her the Clyde. We feel like we have some more profound understanding of the running water and the bridge. I try to climb up to tightrope along the railings. Daize, grinning and with love, drags me back before I can and tells me to "stop being a twat". We buy burgers from a place called the *Bifteki* and demolish them in seconds. We talk about Greg, about Skud, about her dad's death, say the things that need saying without any sadness. It's impossible to stop chatting. We talk all the way back to the hotel room, where we're destined to continue on all through the night.

Greg, still fully clothed, is asleep in the ensuite bathtub. We take turns peeing and brushing our teeth, but he doesn't stir. We get into the double bed together. Daisy nestles in close. We gaze into each other's eyes, whispering as night melts to morning on the other side of the window.

'Why do you want to go to Australia, J?'

'What do you mean?'

'My dad wanted to go there, that's always stuck with me. His little riffs about Australia. Then I heard a girl talk about it in the changing rooms at school. Her sister or cousin or something lived there, and I decided then I was going. It sounded so far away, and I wanted to be far away. That's how I felt tonight.'

'Can't get much further than Australia.'

'None of us are going to Australia. That's what Greg said earlier when you were getting the chips. He said we were never really going.' She nods as if she'd known this all along, letting her eyes close for a moment. When she opens them again, she looks up at me and smiles with her mouth but not her eyes. 'School's almost over, J. And it's all about to change. Nothing can stay the same forever.' I keep looking at her because I don't know what else to do. Then she says: 'I'm not going to Aberdeen University with you guys.'

'What?' Greg and I had already accepted places at Aberdeen. Daize told us that she hadn't heard yet, which was weird, because her grades were always excellent.

'King's College, Goldsmiths and UCL. I've been accepted to all of them, as long as I pass my exams.' We still had to do finals. Greg needed an A in Computing and Bs in his two other subjects, I needed three Bs. Daisy was set to get six As. She took twice as many classes as we did.

'Wait, where?'

'They're in London. I just need to pick one.'

'Does Greg know?'

She looks towards the ensuite. After a moment, she nods.

'He does now.'

TRACK 7: A REFLECTION

JUNAID: It happened at the school disco. More accurately, it *all* happened at the school disco. It was 1990, a year and a half after my awkward smooch with Daisy in the tents down at Cairn Bay beach. It was November. The windows of the school sports hall were thick with condensation. Nervous, sweaty bodies gyrated to the latest pop hits. Greg was glued to the wall.

'How's your Karate, J?'

'Fine. How come?'

'Cowie's been staring at me all night.' I searched out Cowie across the gym hall. Sure enough, there he was, staring. The upturned collar on his jacket is a retro homage to *Grease*.

'I told you not to go near his sister.'

'His sister can snog who she wants.'

'Not according to him she can't.'

'Vogue' by Madonna prompted choreographed embarrassment from the school dance squad. Gelled hair and sharp elbows jutted. Across the hall, Cowie, veins popping from his neck, made a throat-slitting action at Greg.

'He thinks I've shagged her. I bloody well should've since I'm going to get my head kicked in for it.'

'It might not come to that.'

'She wanted to do it. Told me to. But I couldn't. So she made me do this other thing. *Made* me do it, J.'

'Made you do what?'

'Never mind. She just made me, okay?'

'So how has *Cowie* found out if you won't even tell me?'

'She wanted me to take her to the dance. I said no…' It all began to make sense. Greg had been freaked out all week, staying indoors at lunchtime and was first on the school bus at the end of the day.

'So, you didn't want to take her to the dance and she's going to get her brother to beat you up?'

'I know, right? Talk about a raw deal. I should've just taken her.' The dance squad finished their performance, and Dee-Lite's 'Groove is in the heart' bounced into the speakers. Mirror balls sent moonbeams across our bodies. 'He's not the problem. It's the fact that he'll bring the whole football team. If you're there, then at least it'll be more even.'

'Forget it. The next bus back to Cairn Bay is in quarter of an hour. Let's just get out of here.'

It was after 10 PM when we made our break out into the night. Wintry air turned exhalations to steam and made my arms turn to gooseflesh.

'Ho, ho, ho. What do we have here?' That was Neil Cowe, 'Cowie' to most people. There already with four of his mates and us not twenty metres out the door.

'Piss off, Cowie. I'm going home, and I never touched your sister.'

'Not what I heard, Buchan.' Cowie was one of those people with pencil-thin lips on a mouth always turned down at the corners. He also had a perma-tan despite the fact it was

November. Word in the changing rooms was that he slept in his mum's sunbed the way Michael Jackson sleeps in hyperbaric oxygen chambers.

'Ask Louise.'

'It was Louise that told me, you knob.'

'I don't know what she's told you, we had a snog, but it was–'

'So he admits it? Hear that?' Cowie says it loud, accentuating every word 'He shagged my sister. My fourteen-year-old sister.' He said this as if Greg was forty, and not fourteen himself.

Cowie then launched a haymaker. There was no Jackie Chan sound effect when it landed. The sound was more like raw steak dropped on a pavement. Greg pushed Cowie back off the path, toppling him onto the wet grass, and pointed a finger.

'I don't want to fight here, Cowie, but if you touch me again don't expect me to stand and take it.'

Cowie leapt up. Another haymaker. Greg lifted a leg and hoofed him right in the balls. The four flanking footballers flew into action. Two went for Greg's limbs, pulling him onto the ground, the others took one of my arms each. They held and they punched and they kicked. Greg shouted:

'Get him, J.'

I wriggled in the arms of his friends. I had nowhere to go.

Cowie turned his attention to me. 'Leave it, Jarvis.' I was surprised he knew my name. 'This is between me and Buchan.'

Greg looked up from the ground: 'Aye, and your four mates.'

Cowie kicked him again, and he blacked out.

That's when the next thing happened.

A shadow flew through the air, driving a knee into Cowie's ribs and dropping him to the ground. A few punches and scrappy grappling floored the other two. He turned to the ones on me.

'Get off him!'

'Piss off, Skud.' Cowie struggled back up to his feet. 'You're nothing to do with this.'

'He's from Cairn Bay. You touch anybody from Cairn Bay, you have to deal with me.'

'Come on then,' said Cowie, so Skud tackled him again. He hit Cowie a couple of times in the face. I was still trapped by the two midfielders. Greg was out for the count by that point. Skud, straddling Cowie, had a handful of t-shirt in one hand with his other raised above his head in a fist. I couldn't watch any longer. I closed my eyes tight.

'Hey! What are you little cretins playing at?' It was Mr Robertson the P.E. teacher, surrounded by other teachers who'd drawn the short straw for disco duty. Cowie and his goons dispersed into the wind. Skud was also quick on the move, but before he sprinted off in another direction, he took me by the arm. His grip was firm.

'Never tell anyone, Jun,' he said, fading into the black as quickly as he'd appeared from it.

I went to rouse Greg, as Mr Robertson arrived at our spot on the grass.

'For Christ's sake. We'll need to get him inside and patch him up.' Among the teachers was a goth with dyed hair and Doc Martens. It took me a minute to recognise her from the tent at the Campull. The one I'd had to kiss. The chin.

The three of us ended up in the kitchen behind the hall. Mr Robertson stood with folded arms, his biceps bulging, asking question after question. Miss Duncan dabbed Savlon soaked cotton wool on Greg's face as he sucked air through his teeth. Daisy told the story, or a version of it at least. It was pretty much the truth, but with me in the place of Skud, fending off the guys. I didn't know what she'd seen and what she hadn't. She must've got me mixed up with Skud. Truth is, I'd been anything but brave. But this version of the story worked out better for me. It meant that I didn't have to tell my best friend that I stood there and watched while he got beat up. Greg looked at me, part gratitude, part relief, a sense of brotherhood among the fighters. There I was. The black belt. The coward.

And that's when the last thing happened.

The lights came on. Hippie Patterson, the Modern Studies teacher and DJ, cut the music. Mr Robertson shouted at his football team. Then police were everywhere, and it all went quiet. There was one of those loud feedback noises from the speakers. A policeman shouted at us. Told us that the disco was over, and we were not to go anywhere.

'Everyone's getting searched, so line up.'

Somebody shouted, 'What's this about?'

'We know there are drugs in here, and whoever has them is going to wish they'd never been born.' I thought of Skud's parting words. One of Cowie's friends made a run for the fire exit and was tackled by another officer. Mini-skirted girls screamed. Others cried. Football players stood with hunched shoulders and guilty faces. Mr Robertson's tattoos glowed on his forearms. The officer in the DJ booth yelled at us.

'Nobody move or I'll arrest the bloody lot of you, and you'll be in a cell till Monday morning!'

'DRUGS RAID AT LOCAL SCHOOL DISCO' was the headline in the *Invergowan Herald*. Along with the one that affected me the most: 'Invergowan TEEN DIES IN BATHTUB'. Skud was staying at his dad's house at the time. He was constantly passed back and forth between his parents. His dad was a fisherman, and spent most of the time at sea, so Skud's body wasn't found for two days.

When I heard that he'd died, I sank into disbelief. In that surreal, post-death blur, the school went quiet and the assembly on Monday morning held a one-minute silence. People wrote messages about Skud on the walls of the toilet cubicles. Teary girls hugged in the hallways.

I was so angry.

How dare he die.

How dare he die so easily.

FAITH

TRACK 8: THE DROWNING MAN

GREGOR: I woke up in the bathtub of the B&B. I had a mental headache. Snippets of the night before started coming back. Losing the championship to that twelve-year-old dick-bag. Drinking pitcher after pitcher. Daisy and J marching me out of the pub. I was embarrassed. Heartbroken.

I can see it all happening. The visuals are there, but the audio is hazy. Daize and J took an arm each, but I've no idea what they said because I was too busy puking on J's gi, Daisy's boots, and a motorway far below us. Daisy dressed me back into my normal clothes. I can hear the tone of their voices, but not the words, as they figured out what to do with me. J was loud. Daisy was quiet. But once they got me into the B&B, I must've blacked out.

I got out of the bathtub, drank straight from the tap, and had a shot of mouthwash. Staring at my pale face in the mirror, I figured it was better *not* to know what had been said. I came out into the room to find Daisy snuggled up into J's shoulder and I wondered what that meant.

I decided not to argue at seven in the morning. Still half-drunk and confused, I got my stuff and left. I wasn't ready to face Daisy. I needed to give myself a chance to remember the night before. And I definitely wasn't about to accuse her of doing anything with J, not when he was still in the room. She hated me being jealous. I asked them both on separate occasions later. Did you? J laughed in my face before asking if I was serious. Daisy went mental, adding it to the growing list of reasons why she wants to call it quits.

After three and a half years together, that's the language she uses: "call it quits".

And yet, I continue to make an arse of myself.

I phone, I write letters, I turn up in the middle of the night. I try flowers, balloons, and Cure memorabilia.

'Daize, please. You can't throw away three years because I got drunk.'

'You don't remember, do you?'

'Remember what? I was hammered. Whatever happened, it was the drink, not me.'

'Or the truth coming out.'

I begged. Got on my knees and clung to her.

'Daize. I'll do anything. I swear. I'll never enter another *Street Fighter* competition.'

'Greg–'

'I'll get a real job. I'll, I'll sell my consoles for the Australia fund.'

She went quiet then.

'It's too late, Greg. There's no coming back from this.'

'It's never too late.'

'It's so far past being late. And all this crap about sleeping with J? J! He's your best friend. What do you think I am? *Who* do you think I am? You obviously don't know a thing about either of us.'

'I screwed up, okay. I admit that. But you screwed up too. You should've told me about uni. But we can still figure it out, Daize. We've made it this far, we can make it through this.'

We've had the same conversation fifty times.

The night of the championships hasn't come back into focus. But I do remember the sound bite that Daisy's upset about. I can't bring myself to claim it though, to admit to having said it. That would be banging nails into the coffin. But I also remember another thing. What I was going to do if I won the competition. And I still want to ask that question. Now more than ever. If I show renewed commitment to our relationship, she might give us another chance.

I take the virtual reality headset back for a refund and spend the thousand quid on a ring. The diamond is tiny but perfect. I have to try. Sometimes you need to have faith, even when it feels like you're drowning.

I put the box with the ring in my inside pocket and leave for the party.

TRACK 9: THE FUNERAL PARTY

DAISY: The party's in one of the newer suburbs on the outskirts of Invergowan, all fishermen and oil rig workers. The large houses have huge BMWs, not to mention well-stocked drinks cabinets. With mams and dads on holiday, the left-behinders are making the most of it. The party has a mixture of people from different cliques at school. It's got more like that as life as we know it, and exams, have come to an end. I pour a pint of wine.

It's Aileen Hendry's house. Remember her? From Guides? She's going to Edinburgh Uni to do a degree in German. First, though, she's off to spend a month in Germany before her course starts. Seems like everybody's trying to get out of this place. She plans to "ficken, poppen, rammeln the boys". Feisty as ever that one, and long past stopping guys at second base. We play a drinking game involving tequila shots. The reason for pints of wine, tequila, and the one-way train to oblivion, is Greg. I know he's coming, so he's either found out, or he'll find out soon. I doubt I could say it all sober, anyway. But that's also 'cause he's been a nightmare the last couple of months. Turning up in the middle of the night, disrupting my study sessions in the library, never letting up. I'll kill him if I fail my exams.

Aileen downs a tequila then sucks on a wedge of lime.

'Your turn, Daize. Line them up.' The bottle's nearly finished, and I get the worm. I lick the salt, choke back the booze, and gulp down the Mexican beastie. The doorbell goes, and it's the boys. I suck hard on my wedge of lime.

It makes my face screw up.

JUNAID: Daize gives me an awkward at-a-distance hug as if to show Greg that we never slept together in Glasgow. He asked me about it once, and I burst into nervous laughter. He wasn't kidding around though. I told him he'd know that we were fully clothed in that B&B if he'd bothered to hang around or looked under the covers. Explained that we'd been up most of the night, drunk and chatting about exams. I didn't say anything about the nightclub, or what happened outside of it. He'd asked about the B&B, not the rest of the evening, but there's only so far you can stretch the truth before it snaps. He went off on a different tangent then, asking what we'd spoken about, looking for details to comb through. As always, I'm stuck in the middle.

'Jaaaaayyyyyyyy. My bestest pal. I haven't seen your pretty wee face in ages.' Daisy avoids eye contact with Greg as she makes it through her awkward hellos. Wavy hair spills onto her favourite Cure t-shirt, an album cover of *Disintegration*. Liner sharpens her eyes, and stripy socks poke out the ends of her jeans. Her red eyes are half-shut. Not a good start.

'Hey, Daize.'

'J, J, Jaaaay, came to the partaaaay. Check me out. I'm a poet, and I know it.' She continues to warble away, still avoiding Greg's eyes. He's sweating already, cheeks patchy-red above his beard.

'Daize,' he says.

'Gregor,' she replies, still not looking.

'You going to speak to me tonight? I've got something to ask you.'

'Not now, Greg, eh? I'm a bit busy at the moment.' She folds huffy arms. Nobody speaks. Perma-tan-Cowie pokes his head out from behind the living room door.

'That you, Greg? We've a Mega Drive and *Mortal Kombat II* in here.' The fight with Cowie at the school disco feels like years ago. 'C'mon and show us why you're the gaming world champion.' Greg takes a lingering look at Daize, then looks at me, expecting me to follow.

'I'll sort us out drinks and be through in a sec.' He clumps his way to the living room, hands deep in his pockets. Daisy follows him with evil eyes:

'Aye, away and play Mega Drive with a face like thunder, see if it ruins my evening. Nothing'll ruin my evening.' Crinkle frown. 'Tell him if he starts his crap then I'm going straight home, J. That, or phoning the cops to get him booted out. I'm not standing for it tonight. This is *my* party.'

GREGOR: I hate these things. People drinking cheap booze out of tins and plastic cups. Fag butts in empty cans. Bowls of crisps that too many people have had their hands in. And all these strangers. I mean, I know their names. Most of them. They've been in some of my classes at school, but it's not like we're friends. So why all come to the same house to clique it up in kitchens and hallways? There are two answers:

1/. It's the end of school, and I get that.

and:

2/. People are looking for hook ups.

I'm not here for either.

Cowie blabs about how I'm a world champion as if he's my best mate and we've never had any problems. He pats J on the back when J brings drinks.

This is not how I planned it. It's hardly the ideal situation–Daisy off her face–but I have to at least try. I check to see if the ring is still safe in my pocket. It is.

A few rounds of ripping people to bits in *Mortal Kombat*'ll prove I'm not here to ruin her night. Anyway, I need her to sober up first. I grab a controller and select Kung Lao. A guy I've never met has the other controller and plays Johnny Cage.

'Hey, did you win the *Street Fighter* World Championships?'

I don't take my eyes off the game.

'Three times.'

The TV groans, 'FINISH HIM!' and Kung Lao uses his razor-rimmed hat to slice Johnny Cage in half. Johnny splits down the middle and collapses in a spray of blood.

DAISY: He's been on the computer for what feels like hours. I waltz in, explain that this is supposed to be a party, and pull the plug of the Mega Drive from the wall. When I put on 'Push' from the Cure's 1985 album, *The Head on the Door*, the boys whinge. But when the volume's turned up, and the music gets going, they relax. Getting into party mode, they crack cans of lager, and try their best chat up lines on any female willing to listen.

A girl nobody knows starts to sing.

Greg scowls at me, and I scowl right back. I should tell him, now, loud and in front of everybody. But I'm classier than that, better than that, and Greg deserves better than that too. I straighten up. It's a helicoptery feeling.

Later.

I need to sober up first.

I hit the kitchen for food to soak up the drink. I put a couple slices of bread into the toaster and munch Cheesy Wotsits while I'm waiting.

'Daize, can we speak yet?' The sound of his voice hunches up my shoulders. 'It's not the usual stuff. It's different.' The

Cure is switched to a rubbish Oasis song in the living room. The lyrics are gobbledegook. These Gallagher lads are no Robert Smith, that's for sure. I do a ten-tonne sigh as I get cream cheese out from the fridge.

'Come on then, let's hear it.'

'It's just–'

'Aye.'

'I wanted to–' Aileen comes into the kitchen. 'Sorry, Aileen, could you give us a minute? I need to ask Daize something.'

Aileen starts to leave.

'Wait, Aileen. You can say what you need to say in front of her.' Aileen's been good to me since the split.

'I can't, Daize.'

'And I can't be arsed with the same conversation, Greg. Over and over.' I'm empowered with Aileen being there. 'D'you know what? I've got something to tell *you,* actually. It's got nothing to do with games consoles. Still want to hear it?' I pause, prepare to say the four little words I've been practising for the last two weeks. Greg looks defeated already. One last breath, and then: 'I'm going to Australia.'

Take that.

'I know, but I've a–'

'No. Ha! No, Greg. That's where you're wrong. See. Cause I leave on Monday morning.' I check the clock on the microwave, do the sums. 'Fifty-six hours and I'm out of here.' Now I see the look I was expecting. 'That's right. Exams are done. We're free. I cleaned out the old dear's savings account, it's my money anyway, isn't it? She's spent her share and it's my turn, Greg. It's my turn to–' I start to choke up but catch myself. 'It's my money, and I need to. It's been. And I'm–'

The tears come then, the bastards. I turn and try to spread the cream cheese on my toast, but I can't use my hands. Tears spot the worktop and drop into the cheese tub. Greg takes the knife and starts to spread my toast for me, and I can't stop it then. I wail. He drops the knife and pulls me into a hug.

'Okay,' he says. 'It's okay.'

JUNAID: Aileen's got her hands on her hips, looking at Daisy's head in the toilet bowl. Daize hit the booze hard after Greg left. I've no idea what they said to each other.

'We'll leave her in here, my folks're in Tenerife for another week. She can sleep in their bed once she's puked it all up.' Aileen turns to Daisy and shouts, in the belief that being drunk makes you deaf, 'YOU CAN SLEEP IN HERE, DAISY. ALL RIGHT, CHUM? GET IT ALL UP BEFORE YOUR FLIGHT ON MONDAY.' Daisy's head's still in the bowl, but she gives a thumbs up sign and spits. I take Aileen by the arm and turn her around.

'Flight? What flight?'

'Daisy's flight. She's going to Australia on Monday.'

I take a few seconds to register this.

'Since when?'

'Since ages. Why do you think we're having a party?'

'DAIZE? IS THAT TRUE? WHY DIDN'T YOU SAY SOMETHING?' I don't know why I copy Aileen's shouting. Daisy's three feet away.

'Leave me alone, J. I just need to puke for a bit.' I'm more than tipsy myself by this point and struggle to process this new information. That must've been the focus of Daize and Greg's deep and meaningful earlier.

Aileen drags me to the kitchen to make toast, then to the living room to play *Mortal Kombat*. She grabs a controller and challenges me to a match, a slice of toast with cream cheese hanging from her mouth. She uses the character Kitana, standing up to play while I flop onto the couch. I select Johnny Cage and proceed to kung-fu her. But it's hard to focus on the game. I can't help but wonder how Greg and I are the last to know that Daisy's leaving the country on Monday. Monday! We hadn't spoken about Australia since Glasgow. "We were never really going." I don't know what my face is doing, but Aileen says:

'Ach. Quit sulking, Jarvis. That ship's sailed.'

My cheeks flush. 'What are you on about?'

'What am I on about? It's written all over your face. She's going to the other side of the planet to get away from all of this. You and your chum included.'

Aileen's stopped following our match, so I make Johnny Cage slap her. After a few more punches and kicks, he rips her torso off her legs, expressing my feelings perfectly. Aileen laughs at the screen, then looks at me a bit sexy.

'That's the first time a guy's ripped me in half.'

'Did you like it?'

'I can think of worse ways to spend the evening.'

The door of Aileen's bedroom slams shut behind us. She dives on to me, hooking an unexpectedly flexible leg halfway up my back. She tries to kiss me with her big red mouth, but I move my head. There's a greasy dollop of cream cheese smeared up her left cheek.

'Shouldn't we get to know each other first?'

'Das ist mir scheißegal,' she says, fumbling at my belt and zipper. Her creamy visage leans in for another attempted kiss. I push her away. 'Mmmm-hmmm, sind sie versuchen, mich zu necken? Playing the tease is it?'

'I might be.' I'm *literally* trying to avoid the cream cheese.

She moves back, fixing me with her sexiest stare. She then prowls to her bedside cabinet, producing a set of furry handcuffs, the kind you get at bachelorette parties.

'Sitzen,' she commands, motioning to the chair near the desk. She points to the zip on her dress. 'Aufmachen.'

'Sorry?'

'Aufmachen. Open!'

I do as I'm told, revealing a matching blue bra and knickers. I catch Aileen's scent, a mix of orange soap and spicy perfume. She turns back to me, shimmies out of the dress. This development removes all concern with her cream cheese topping. She prowls towards me with the handcuffs.

'Let's see if I can get Daisy Parker out of your head.'

On the way downstairs, I peep into what must be Aileen's little sister's bedroom. Barbie and Ken are on the wallpaper, curtains, and the "wedding day" duvet cover. The pink lampshade shines its glow on a thousand plastic dolls stacked in neat rows in a cabinet on the back wall. Cowie is top to tail on the single bed with David Oliver, a guy I sat next to in fourth year biology. The dolls watch on. Wide-eyed and hang-jawed, they observe the angles of grinding flesh. I shut the door as quick as I opened it, but the guys haven't noticed me, engaged in their own biology lesson.

When I get to Daize, she's watching *Eurotrash* on Channel 4. Antoine de Caunes and Jean Paul Gaultier are chatting with Austrian porn stars. I throw her a bag of Maltesers.

'I just saw Cowie and David Oliver. I'm pretty sure they were–'

'Shagging? They do that every weekend,' she says with a didn't-everyone-know-that? flippancy. Her hair is scraped back into a ponytail, the make-up washed from her face.

'Really?'

'Yup,' she says, popping a *Malteser* in her mouth, her lips pouting as she sucks at the chocolate. She crunches into it. 'I feel like crap.'

'You look like crap,' I lie, still stuck to the door frame.

'Thanks, friend. Can you close the door? I'm not sure I'm allowed to be in here.' I do as she asks and move nearer to the bed. She pulls back the duvet and pats the space next to her.

When I get in, she holds the bag of Maltesers under my nose, and I take a couple. We're quiet for a bit, crunching down on the sweets. We haven't hung out much since Glasgow. And for the last month we've been on exam leave, so haven't been in school a lot either, but it's like we haven't missed a beat. She goes first:

'I don't understand this programme, why do they voice everyone over to sound like Devon farmers?' She looks young without her make-up on, and I try to remember the old Daisy's face, from before her operation.

'It's supposed to be funny. Like they're normal people, even if it's a famous porn star or something.'

'It's not funny.'

'Change the channel.'

'Nah. It's easy on the brain.'

I nod in sarcastic sympathy. We lie in bed, as straight as steamrollers, quilt tucked up under our armpits.

'So. Australia, eh?'

'Yup.'

'On Monday.'

'Yup.'

'*Shit*, Daize.'

'Aye.' She mutes *Eurotrash* and turns to face me, getting comfy in her pillows. She doesn't look like crap at all. Not considering she threw up a few hours ago. The colour is back in her cheeks, the twinkle back in her eyes. 'I've been planning since Glasgow. I'm going out on a tourist visa till I turn eighteen. Then I'm going to switch it to a working holiday visa and stay for a year.' Yet another sentence that I need a moment to process.

'A year.' I stumble. 'What about uni?'

'I accepted a place at King's College in London, but I've deferred starting until next September.'

'Oh. That's…I mean…A *year*? It's great, Daize. It's what you always wanted. I just can't believe you're telling me, telling *Greg*, a couple of days before you leave.'

'I know. I'm sorry, J. I really am. But I didn't want to give anybody the chance to change my mind. I had to wait till the last minute.'

'How did he take it?'

'You know what he's like.' I nod. 'At least you shouldn't have to worry about that stuff with us in the B&B. He brought it up again, but only 'cause he's looking for some specific thing he can blame. It's his way of coping. He's getting better though, I think. We managed to have a civil conversation for the first time in weeks. I'm going to meet him tomorrow, and we'll spend part of the day together. I need to say goodbye to his mam and dad. I grew up in that house.'

'Yeah.'

She thinks for a moment. 'I just need to go, J. I can't begin to explain how much.' She smiles. 'I've missed you, you know.'

'I've missed you too.'

It's quiet for a while then. We watch the muted TV and finish the chocolates.

'Do you think I could still come?' She gives me a funny look. 'I don't know what to do anymore. After school, I thought things were going to feel different. But I'm more confused than ever. I know I've got a place at Aberdeen University, but, *Business Studies*? What even *is* Business Studies? What am I going to do? Sell microwaves? And I'm not sure I want to live in Aberdeen either. I applied because I thought we were all applying.' She looks heartbroken, and I backtrack. 'Sorry. That sounds selfish. But, how do you know what you're supposed to study, or where you're supposed to live? Now that school's ending, I don't know where to start. I'm lost, Daize.' If I was the kind of person who cried, I might've cried at this point. But I won't allow tears to form in my eyes.

'Oh, J,' she says. I look at Daisy's still-new face. She smiles. 'I don't know what I'm supposed to do either. But I know that whatever it is, I need to do this next bit alone. You can visit, once I'm settled, but I–'

'It's okay. I know. I'll visit. I'll come for a holiday.'

'Promise?'

'Promise.'

'Thanks for understanding. Anyway, somebody needs to stay and watch over Greg for a while. I'm not sure how he's going to cope after…'

'After what?'

'Later. You'll find out later.'

We share a moment that we know signals the end of something. But at least we have the next few hours in bed before everyone else gets up. And I know that those hours will pass like seconds. I can't numb the feeling of sadness, so I decide to change the topic.

'I shagged Aileen.'

Daize bites the inside of her lips in an attempt to conceal her smile.

'That's great!'

'She had cream cheese on her face the whole time.'

Daisy laughs so hard she snorts.

GREGOR: She said no, which I suppose you figured out. Closed her hand over the box so she didn't have to look at the ring. She didn't even want to see what I'd chosen. That was hard, but then she was leaving so soon, what could I do? Be angry? Or love her? Love her like I've always loved her? So that's what I did. I told jokes, said that the diamond was fake anyway. It's not. Nothing I've ever given to Daisy Parker has been fake.

PORNOGRAPHY

TRACK 10: THE HANGING GARDEN

JUNAID: Japanese announcements echo around the airport. I remember the announcements in London and mock-translate: 'Japan warns that ginger bearded Scotsmen are considered a threat. They will be removed and destroyed'. A sign on the wall reads "Welcome to Japan". The sign is in English and "Kanji", the characters which form the Japanese writing system. I knew we were coming to Japan, but I hadn't thought about the look and sound of the Japanese language.

When we've collected our bags and gone through security, there's a short, bald guy in a grey suit waiting for us. An American amongst the Japanese. Everyone is Japanese. Now Greg is as much an ethnic minority as I am (though, as a ginger, I suppose he was a kind of minority already). The bald guy has a sign that says: "*TEMPLE WARRIOR*." Greg doesn't straighten his back or puff out his chest like he did at the *Street Fighter* competition. Even though he's going to be on Japanese TV.

Greg stays quiet.

The Tufted Duck Hotel is the pride of our village. To rephrase without lying, it's the only pub, so it's where people go to get pissed. It's a two-storey grey rectangle with twenty bedrooms and deaf Joyce Strachan on reception. What else do we have? A chip shop and a post office (which is technically the back of Anne the post lady's house). That's it. That's the amenities in Cairn Bay. According to the brochure, the Hotel Okura's got 833 rooms over 122,000 square metres of space. There're swimming pools inside and out, eight restaurants, three bars, thirty banquet halls, a spa, four wedding parlours, a travel agency, a photo studio, a shopping arcade, a nursery and a dentist. The Imperial suite's 354 square metres, has two bedrooms, a dining room, and an office. It's made for royalty and costs four thousand British Pounds *a night*.

Geishas wearing pink kimonos work at reception. The bell boys wear suits and treat us like we're Prime Ministers. They smile and bow and clasp their hands, then whisk us up to our room. At the Tufted Duck, you're lucky if Joyce has noticed you coming in.

We're set up in a Junior Suite that's nicer than my house. The room's sixty square metres of cream, beige and chocolate brown. Everything matched and picked by the finest interior designers. There are two double beds and an adjoining living area with couches and a TV. There's a bowl of fresh fruit on the table and a fridge with soft drinks and champagne. Also, there are origami swans on our pillows. The room smells like peaches and cream. The window's a panorama of Tokyo, lit up in a rainbow of lights that pulse on buildings as far as the eye can see. It all looks and feels like a dream. I ache to explore it.

Greg locks himself in the bathroom.

'Irasshaimase!'

I kak myself when the restaurant staff scream as we enter. Bill tells us that it's a traditional welcome and it'll happen everywhere we go. Our group has Scots, French, Americans and Russians. We get a few looks, but nothing threatening. Alien smells fill the air, mixed with the more familiar scent of seafood, which reminds me of home. The restaurant's wooden tables appear low but are dug out underneath. Orange and red décor burn with the heat of the kitchen, and the dozens of bodies packed tight at the tables. Scrolls and lanterns hang on the walls. Men and women in sharp business dress clink Sapporo beer bottles with musical toasts. Once we're settled, Bill, the American guy who picked us up at the airport, tells us how he came to work for Irata.

'I came to Japan on the JET Programme. Do you guys know JET?' Head shakes. 'It's a programme for teaching school kids English and a little Western culture. That was eight years ago. I stayed on the programme for three years in a town called Takeo, down south. I'd been to Tokyo a bunch and wanted to try living here, so I went for an internship with Irata. I've lived here ever since. I love it. I love my job, and I'm still fascinated by Japan. The culture, the people.' He sips his beer, as we stare on in admiration. 'This is the first time Irata have done anything like this. Video games are still a new venture for us, so excuse me if I don't know what I'm doing. My job description is to make sure you guys are comfortable, so if you need anything, gimme me a holler.'

We're all jealous that Bill has scored the coolest job in the world, and are in awe when he orders for us in fluent Japanese. I want to know more but am scared to ask in front of all these strangers. How hard is it to learn the language? Why does he stay? Can anybody do the JET Programme? I feel as though I've something deeper in common with him. He talks us through the sushi; makizushi, futomaki, nigirizushi and inarizushi. These names mean nothing to me, but I love the sound they make on my tongue. The food arrives as it's ready, in colourful parcels of fish, vegetables, egg and tofu. I thought sushi was raw fish, I had no idea of the variety; the salmon rolls and fried tofu are my favourites. One of the Russians, Elena, adds thick clumps of wasabi to her soy sauce and tells us to try it. She laughs as we all rush to our drinks to numb our hot mouths.

Greg didn't come with us for dinner.

The next day we're brought to Shibuya in a chauffeur-driven Toyota. The streets bubble and pop with office workers (known as "salarymen" and "office ladies") as well as gambling addicts and kids skipping school. As we're ushered into the biggest arcade I've ever seen, Bill says:

'Sixty minutes on the clock. Go wild.'

There are five levels. The bottom floor is full of grabby-grabby machines. The ones with the big claws that you use to snatch yourself a prize. They're called "UFO Catchers" here. Seven-foot-tall Perspex rectangles with pink neon strips along the top. They chirp theme songs and entice punters with more than teddies. Schoolgirls in heels that defy gravity try to win designer make-up and handbags. Computer geeks aim for figurines of their favourite busty anime characters.

On the second floor are the infamous pachinko machines. Their balls tinkle next to screens showing clips of what looks like a Japanese soap opera. Mah-jong machines with strippers hold the attention of dishevelled salarymen. The place is almost full. At ten o'clock. On a Wednesday morning. The air smells of pine needles and cigarettes. Floor three is Greg's territory. *Street Fighter*'s calls of '*Round One, FIGHT!*' combine with screeching cars and machine gun fire. The sounds of Greg's childhood. It's rammed. A too-pretty couple with platinum hair and tight black clothing sit at a car racing game. The girl on the boy's lap, cigarettes smoked in synchronised puffs. Rows of boys with headphones bet on computerised horse races. Anyone could be in here. Everyone is in here. Except for Greg.

Greg refused to leave the hotel.

DAISY: We almost broke up before, loads of times, but that was kids' stuff. Once, when I was young and stupid (I know I'm *still* young and stupid), I told him I was pregnant. I thought he would flip, lose it, tell me to get rid of "the baby". But that's not Greg. I didn't know him then like I do now. He went the opposite way, said we could get married, that I could move in. I told him I was joking, and he went in a mood for a week. But while he believed it, he was beautiful. In that protective Greg mode. Greg steps up; he never shies away. I knew then he would never, ever hurt me. That he was safe. But sometimes the things that you love about somebody are the things that end up pushing you away from them.

Don't think that any of this was flippant or easy. It wasn't. Seeing somebody you love get down on one knee and bring a box out was heartbreaking. My sixteen-year-old goth self was sure that's what the future would be for us. But we've gone too far past that. I couldn't bear to see the ring. I stopped him when he went to open the box. I didn't want it to be exactly how I'd imagined.

Coming here wasn't easy either. I had a picture in my head about what things would be like on the other side of the world, but the reality was different. At the airport, I asked the taxi driver to take me to a hotel with a view of Sydney harbour. I booked myself into an overbudget room and burst into tears. It all came out then. All the stuff I'd pushed down, tucked away, about my folks, about getting away from Greg. I'd no idea if I'd done the right thing. I've still got no idea. I spent those first few days in overpriced luxury. I read Sylvia Plath and wrote jetlagged letters at the window, wishing I'd never come to Australia. I didn't know anybody and what the hell was I actually going to do for the next year of my life? It was the end of the make-believe.

I got through it by telling myself that I just needed a few days to get my head together. That I didn't need to think about the next year, finding a job, a house, flatmates, or any of that stuff. I could have a holiday first, a break. I walked around the area near the hotel and asked at the reception about the harbour. I took pictures of the opera house with a disposable camera, took a bus to another neighbourhood. Baby steps. I definitely wasn't ready to jump right into hostelling the length and breadth of the country. I was terrified of bunk-bedding it with dreadlocked German drug dealers. Sorry hostels. (We've made up). I slept a lot, trying to get in sync with Oz-time. I ate pancakes for breakfast and chips for all other meals. I spent a full month's budget during my week-long stay in that hotel, and it was worth every penny. By the end of it, I'd stopped crying. Felt more like myself. Sydney wasn't so scary.

I got a travel diary from my mam before I left. After I'd guilt-tripped her into giving me the contents of her bank account, I wasn't expecting a gift. I loved it and carried it everywhere. I wrote snippets that would become my *Bell Jar*, my *Orlando*, my *Frankenstein*. I started with descriptions of the Sydney Opera house. They included "space-age shells" and "futuristic arcs". And, in the evening, "throbbing light, like a UFO". Maybe I'd be better at sci-fi than travel writing? Still, I forced myself to write a page every day.

I switched to a hostel at the end of the first week. This was for my bank balance more than anything, but I still had no inclination to find work. I spent the mornings on Bondi beach or cycling Sydney back streets on a hostel-borrowed bike. Afternoons involved galleries and reading dog-eared novels in shady cafes. It was eighteen degrees, but compared to Scotland, that's positively roasting. There're fewer ginger people in

Sydney than in Scotland, but every time I saw one, there was Greg on one knee. And there were the guilts again.

I hope he's okay.

Sydney doesn't know who Greg is though, and the city bubbles with sun, sea, sand, surf and sex. I'd no desire to take part in any sex at this point. But the amount of bed-hopping that went on in the hostel suggested that it wouldn't be hard to find willing partners. So with sex off limits, and with sun, sea and sand mastered quickly, there was one thing left to conquer. The one goal that stood out above the others and the real reason I came in the first place.

I was going to surf.

THE TOP

TRACK 11: GIVE ME IT

JUNAID: It went like this. When Daisy left, I was on take-care-of-Greg duty. I was happy to be. Daisy and I had talked through everything we needed to talk through, and now she was gone. Greg and I only had each other. I knew that her first few weeks away would be the hardest, especially around her birthday, so I took him on holiday. I bought us tickets to *GamesMaster Live,* a video games show that was touring around the major UK cities. We took off for ten days, going to the expo in Manchester, Glasgow, and Edinburgh. It didn't magically solve anything, there were lots of quiet train and bus rides, but it helped. Being on the move, being busy, was good for both of us. And better for Greg than sitting in his bedroom pretending that things were fine. Best of all was discovering the Irata PKD, a new video games console from Japan. Greg fell in love with the PKD's top title, a game called *Temple Warrior*. On our way to the expo for the second time, he spoke about getting hold of a PKD on import, but he didn't need to, in the end.

GREGOR: I fell in love with it. It was ages since I'd been excited about anything. I even thought about selling the engagement ring to get one on import, but I didn't need to, in the end. After the second visit to *GamesMaster Live,* I already knew what was going to happen.

We went for the third and final time in Edinburgh. The Irata workers dismantled the stall in the same way I'd seen them do it twice before. The PKD consoles were in plastic cabinets so that people couldn't touch them. The wires for the control pads came through holes in the front. They got velvet-gloved into padded bags by the Irata guys. Wires pulled, controllers put into bubble-wrap bags. I now knew exactly how each component would be tucked away.

I waited until the closest guy moved onto the next console along, and his pal went to the opposite side of the stand. At the split second when they were both occupied, I picked up one of the packed PKDs. I slipped the strap of the bag over my shoulder, and walked towards J, who'd been off having his hourly protein shake. I started him towards the door.

'We're leaving.'

'Leaving? There's still a couple–'

I grabbed him by the upper arm to drag him.

'Act natural.'

'*Me* act natural? What the hell's going on?'

'I've nicked a PKD.'

'What?'

I dragged him to the exit, letting go of his arm so we could leave casually. I gave a wee nod to the staff: 'Thanks now, bye'. A glance back at the stall told me nobody'd noticed yet. Outside I lost my cool, bolting into the first car at the taxi rank. J followed at my heels, jumping in and closing the door.

I pointed ahead and said 'go, go, go!' to the Driver.

'Go, go, go where, pal?'

'Away from here. Go.'

'Listen, mate, I can't drive unless you tell me where I'm going.'

'What's the name of the station, J?'

'Um. Waverly?'

'Waverly station, please.'

'Right then, now we can "go, go, go" can't we?' He pulled off, and the meter clicked. I checked out the back window. Nobody was looking for a shifty gamer who'd nicked a grand's worth of console not due out in the UK for another year.

JUNAID: Greg was far from on the mend, but at least he had something new to focus on. It's like they say, "you can take the person out of the game, but you can't take the gamer out of the person". Okay, nobody actually says that, but Greg had a new obsession, which made him more like Greg again. He stopped working at the Co-op and played *Temple Warrior* on his nicked PKD as if it were a full-time job.

With Daisy gone and Greg somewhat occupied, I had my own regime. It involved lots of right hooks on the punch bag in my garage. I aimed for five thousand a day. The bag has a dent where I connect, and the rafters wobble each time. I took a self-defence course which focussed on realistic situations and philosophical concepts. I began to relearn my old Karate forms using a book I got for my birthday years ago. I went through the movements in the garage, pretending that I was beating up bad guys. The steps, punches and kicks slowly came back to me. I've spent too much of my life relying on Greg and Daisy to fight my battles, hiding behind their friendship. I tried to live *through* their relationship so that I didn't have to face my own demons. Even if I wanted to keep doing that, it's not an option now, is it? Daisy's gone, and Greg needs me to step up and be the strong one for a while, so that's what I'm doing.

I definitely feel more independent since doing the self-defence course. I know how to take care of myself, but I still need to figure out what to do with my life. On my days off from ScotMart, I work shifts in my uncle's factory. I've spent a few weekends picking strawberries on a local farm for extra cash too. With summer ending, none of these jobs feels like a long-term option. But then, neither does Business Studies at Aberdeen University.

GREGOR: Mam brought the portable handset into my bedroom. I still expect that phone calls will be Daisy. But she hadn't phoned since she got to Australia. Must be J then.

'J?'

'Hello? May I speak with Mr Gregor Buchan, please.'

'Oh. Eh. Speaking.'

'Hello, Mr Buchan. My name is Bill Washburn. I'm calling on behalf of the Irata Corporation, Japan.'

Dickbags.

JUNAID: Two scoops of protein powder go into the shaker, and I top it up with full-fat milk. I do this three times a day on top of meals based on protein-packed meats. I wondered if I was going to get podgy. But according to the guy in the Sports shop, it'd be impossible for this to happen with the amount that I'm training. Turns out he's right. I don't gain that much weight at all, but the shape of my body is definitely changing.

There are no love handles to pinch, and my chest has firmed into proud pecs. I'm not Bruce Lee yet, but if I stand under the bathroom light, you can pick out my four-and-a-half-pack abs. A six-pack is closer every day. Right after a training session is the best time to get under the light. Veins pop from pumped biceps and forearms. There's even a vein that runs across the top left abdominal muscle. My arms and shoulders have changed the most, they have thickened up and widened out. I'm now more of a square than a gangly rectangle. Every t-shirt I own is getting tight. In a good way.

It'd been months since I met the neds on the bridge, and it would be a different story if I met them now. My five thousand right hooks a day will soon see me break the half-million mark and I'll hit a million in the New Year. Take all the muscle away, I'd still have my right hook. I can deliver it from six inches and generate knockout power. Put me back on that bridge, and I'd domino-topple the seven dwarfs with ease. Ping, ping, ping. Hook, hook, hook.

'J, get your arse out the bathroom.'

'Greg? What're you doing here?'

'I've been asked to go to Japan.'

'What?'

'I got a call from a guy at Irata.'

'Oh crap! They found out about the PKD?'

'No, nobody found out about the PKD. Can you get out here for a minute?' I opened the bathroom door, towel around my waist. Greg waltzed in and sat on the edge of the bath. 'The PKD comes out in Japan soon, right? And the Irata Corporation's planning this big event that gamers are going mental over.'

'Okay.'

'So, what's their flagship title?'

'I don't know, *Temple Warrior?*'

'Correct. And who's Scottish?'

'Me?'

'No. In *Temple Warrior,* you gimp.'

'Greg, what the hell are you going on about? They want a Scottish person to go to Japan to play *Temple Warrior,* is that it?'

'Exactly. Irata hired some Yakuza henchman to get the best

beat-em-up player from Scotland. They went to the *Street Fighter* Championships. Et voila.'

'But Albert won the *Street Fighter* Championships.'

'Once, J. Albert won them once, and I won them three years in a row.'

'Right.'

'Also, Albert's twelve, and you need to be eighteen. So, Mr Grown Up here was next on the list.'

'Man, Albert must be gutted.'

'Forget Albert, J. I've been winning that championship before he knew *Street Fighter* existed. Anyway, get this. They're flying in the best gamers from France, Russia and the U.S. to play the international characters. So, all the world's top gamers'll be playing in Japan, where video games were born. Well. Kinda. And I've nailed every character on the hardest difficulty level before anybody else can own a PKD. Meaning that I get to complete part of the Master Plan: being crowned the number one gamer on planet Earth.'

'So, this is what happens when you steal.' It was the most animated I'd seen him since Daisy left. The most Greg-like. This was good news, and if I wasn't so happy to see Greg take a step closer to being his former self, I might've even been jealous.

'It gets better. It's all expenses paid.'

'Nice!'

'It gets better still.'

'I doubt it.'

'I'm allowed to bring a friend. And guess who I happen to owe a holiday?'

DAISY: I've hung out with and got to know a few of the staff at the hostel in the few weeks I've been here. Most of the other tourists come and go on their travels, but the staff and I have hung around. One of the receptionists, Helene (German;

dreadlocked; not a drug dealer) tips me off about the competition. We sit out back on her lunch break, eating sandwiches.

'Up at Manly, there'll be competitions for juniors, ladies and the dudes. It'll be on all weekend. Go check it out, it's about an hour away.' Helene speaks pitch perfect Australian-English, sounding exactly like a Sydney native.

'Do they make a lot of money?'

'Less than before. Surfing's going through a rocky patch. It's hard for pros to make a living right now. The competitions don't pay as much prize money as they used to, so a lot of the pros need day jobs. Some are still at school or uni. Others teach surfing, make boards, work in bars, or do other beach activities, legal and not so legal.' She raises a pierced eyebrow and throws the crusts of her sandwiches in the bin. I nod. Would I suit dreadlocks? Skimming over the water with them thrashing about behind. Helene moves to go back to her shift on reception. 'It's fun to watch. Most of the pros are cool too. But if you want to learn, go to one of the surf shops and have lessons already. You've been talking about it since you got here.'

I take the next ferry up to Manly.

I spy her as soon as I get to the beach. Out on the waves as if it's nothing, smiling and waving to other surfers. Her legs and shoulders are toned and strong. Her thrummy brown hair tangled in wet ringlets about her shoulders. I get close when she comes in for a pit stop. She's all fluid movements and perfect teeth, throwing her head back when she bursts into belly laughs. I've never seen anything like her. I'm proud of the tan I'm getting but feel pasty and Scottish compared to the natural cinnamon colour of her skin. Her board says "Coolangatta Queen".

I lose track of her when the junior competition starts. Skinny, frisky boys and girls jive along the sets of waves. Their schoolmates screech and howl from the beachfront. The girl who wins the junior event is twelve. *Twelve*. The announcer says she'll be a future star of the pro circuit. A gangly girl with golden hair and skin. Everything in Australia's golden; the beaches, the sunsets, the people. Her red surf outfit and white board stand out against the blue. She sweeps herself round in long turns or whips round on the spot. Her winning wave sees her lean so far forward that I can't understand how she doesn't come tumbling off her board. Instead, she styles her way along the wave, popping off the end of it with a grin on her face. A smile's plastered on my face too, and my voice is hoarse from shouting.

When the women's competition starts up, I keep my eyes peeled for the Coolangatta Queen. As I hoped, she takes part. I get butterflies when I see her. Her strong brown legs, the way she pops onto her board and struts as if she's in control of the ocean. I whoop from the shore, my heart leaping when her scores come in. She ends up in third place, but for me, she's the clear winner. As I watch her pick up her trophy, I decide to approach her. I feel stupid, but who cares? Nobody knows me. And if I make a tit of myself, it's not like I'll ever see her again anyway. Being abroad is a chance to be a new person. I've changed my face, now I can change something more than the physical. I can be the Australian version of Daisy that I've dreamt about, having left the world behind. Also, I know, *know*, that this person is destined to be my teacher.

She sees me coming from about twenty yards away, eyes locked on her like a crazed stalker. I must look ridiculous, but I don't care. What's the worst that can happen? When I get up close, she speaks first:

'Please tell me I don't owe you money?' she says, flashing her smile.

'You don't owe me money.'

'Thank Christ for that. What's that accent you've got there?'

'Scottish.'

'All right, Scottish. What can I do for ya? Autograph?' Coffee-brown irises twinkle.

'I watched you in the competition. You were like a badass ballerina.' I'd swithered about whether to say that. She throws her head back and cracks up.

'Thanks. I get my fair share of badarse, but I've never been called a ballerina before.' She pops up on her toes, giving me a graceful and effortless twirl. Her body has that relaxed, unforced, I-look-like-this-all-year-round look.

'You seem so light on the waves. It's amazing to watch.'

'Tell it to the sponsors and get us more prize money will ya? My rent's due next week.'

'I've been looking to do a bit of surfing.' *Here it comes. Here I go.*

'Plenty of surf shops up and down the beach. You checked them out?'

'Not yet. I was going to ask if you knew a good one.' *Please, please be a surf teacher.*

'Yeah. It's called Kelly's, and I work there. Best surf teacher on the East coast.' *YESSSS!*

'Is it close by?'

'To here? Aw, yeah. I'd say about nine hundred kilometres.'

Deflation.

'Nine hundred? You don't live in Sydney?'

'Nah. I'm the Coolangatta Queen, aren't I?' she says, and I figure Coolangatta is a place. 'Surf the Gold Coast mostly, down here to visit mates and do this comp. I'll be heading back up tomorrow.' She can see the disappointment in my eyes and seems to be relishing it. A golden, beach-bum male shouts over.

'Chris, you coming or what?'

'Yeah, in a sec.' She turns back to me, 'what's your name?'

'Daisy Parker.'

'Nice to meet you, Daisy Parker. I'm Chris. Tell you what. If you want real surf lessons, you'll find me at Kelly's.' She points at the word Coolangatta on her surfboard. 'Real swell there, not for the faint-hearted. If you make your way up, I'll give you a discount.' She winks, full of confidence, ballerina turning her body and whipping her salty hair. Off she marches. It's a challenge, the way she says it; "*if* you want *real* surf lessons…*if* you make your way up". I go straight to Helene in the hostel and ask her how I get to Coolangatta.

We'll see who's a badarse.

TRACK 12: BANANAFISHBONES

GREGOR: I suppose you think that I should've gone out with J and the other competitors. Gone to the games centres, to Disneyland, to the sumo wrestling. I understand. I would've loved to have done all those things. It's *Japan*! We're here all expenses paid! I get it. But I brought the PKD with me, and my choice is to be in the hotel room practising for the competition. I know everyone else competing will be playing for the first time. I know that I've been playing for months, so they don't stand a snowball's chance in hell of beating me. But this is the difference, remember? The difference between a regular person and somebody like me, an obsessive. And this competition, *televised,* is a chance to get back some of my identity.

I kept the engagement ring. Couldn't bring myself to return it, in the end. I'm still not ready to let it go, the same way I'm not ready to let go of gaming.

But that's just it. I'm afraid I've hit the roof. That everyone's growing up but me. I'm eighteen years old, and I'm terrified of what would happen if I stopped playing video games. I think about it sometimes. That I've clung to games for fear of what lies beyond them. In Japan, in Australia, without my parents, without Daisy. What comes after, when the games stop? I'm not ready to get rid of this engagement ring, and I'll never give up on gaming. Video games've been there from the start, through everything. They're still here after everyone's deserted me. I'm winning this competition, live on Japanese TV, and when I do, I'll win back myself.

DAISY: Kelly's isn't hard to find. On the beachfront at Rainbow Bay, it's a cafe come surf shop with a chilled-out atmosphere. Mixing food, drinks and surfing was always going to be a good business plan. The shop's a two-storey affair, cafe up top and surfboards down below. Orange bunting hangs around the roof. The first day I check it out, Chris isn't there, but a cheery guy tells me she'll be working the next day. I hang out, drink my first legal beer on the terraced cafe and look out towards the sea. A customer refers to the cheery guy as "Kelly"–turns out he owns the place. Kelly's dark hair is greying a little at the temples, but he's not that old, his eyes and his smile are still youthful.

He comes over to see if I need a refill, and I point out the framed pictures of him on the walls. In one photo, he's in the barrel of a wave, touching his hand to the wall of water beside him. In another he's on a longboard, with his arms stretched out and his head and shoulders thrown back. You can almost hear him scream after conquering a beast of a wave. Then there's a teenage Kelly, bronzed and dreamy with a trophy, smiling from cheek to cheek.

'That guy looks familiar.'

'You'll embarrass me looking at those, mate.'

'How old are you in this one?' I ask, pointing at the trophy picture.

'Fifteen. Nearly twenty years ago, that. Where does it all go, eh?' I smile, wondering the same thing. Where did the last six years go? School came and went in a heartbeat, and it's never coming back. 'You gonna take lessons?'

'Aye. Chris said she'd give me a discount.'

'Is that right?' I make an awkward face, hoping I haven't got her into trouble with her boss. But he just laughs. 'She's a good teacher. A lot of the pros can't teach. Being good at surfing and being a good surf teacher are two different things, you know? Chris is awesome at both. You'll be on your feet in no time.' I get butterflies at the thought of being out on the waves. Kelly brings me another beer, gives me the lowdown on the area of Rainbow Bay and Snapper Rocks. He can't resist telling me a couple of his surfing stories either. When Kelly starts up another story, the guys at the bar groan and roll their eyes.

'Never heard this one before, have we boys?'

'Well she hasn't heard it, has she?'

'Lucky for you, love.'

'I don't mind,' I say. And it's true. The atmosphere's friendly, the guys at the bar are winding Kelly up. I take a long draft of my cold beer and settle in for the next surfing tale. I could get used to this place.

Later, I stare out at the ocean, listening to 'Just Like Heaven' from the Cure's 1987 album, *Kiss Me, Kiss Me, Kiss Me*. Kelly, his shift over, walks towards the water with a huge board and a long oar, wearing nothing but boardies. He's tall and lean, super fit in that effortless way that I saw with Chris. I want to look like that. He gives me a nod, and I wave back. I imagine dad as a greying, beardy hippy, listening to *Pet Sounds* on Scratchy the turntable. *In your mid-forties now, old man.* What would he have made of me here, at Snapper Rocks? According to Kelly, it's one of the most famous spots for big wave surfing on the planet, let alone Australia. Watching him get smaller as he paddles out, I wish my dad could've made it here to see this beach, to catch a wave.

The beach is warm, and the air is fresh. I lie back and look at the low cumulus billowing overhead, a floating city above the Earth. Waves lap at the shore. Salt air fills my nostrils with the smell of home. Robert Smith's lyrics fill my head with their dreamy introspection. I close my eyes and think of surfing. My feet move at the ankle as I imagine gliding along a wave like Kelly's pictures on the cafe walls. When I fall asleep, I dream of dad and surf and mam and Invergowan beach. I'm under for ten minutes before that jerky falling thing happens, and I startle myself awake.

Chris is sitting next to me.

'Daisy Parker. I suppose this means you want a discount?'

JUNAID: Space Mountain. That was my favourite. It's a roller coaster, but it's in the dark. You fly along at a million miles an hour, going up and up and round and down. But because you're blind on this ride, you've no idea what's coming next.

THE HEAD ON THE DOOR

TRACK 13: THE BABY SCREAMS

JUNAID: 'Greg, you need to come out.'

'J. I don't *need* to do anything.'

'We've been in Japan for the best part of a week, and you haven't left the hotel room.'

'And you know the reason. This is important to me, J. This is a chance to be somebody again.'

I don't say anything about his comment, but Greg's expectations for this competition are way out of it. Winning isn't going to make everything go back to the way it was. Daisy is still in Australia. Besides, there's another reason he has to come out for dinner.

'I know. But it's not about that. It's Bill.'

'What about Bill?'

'He didn't say it in so many words, but basically, you *have* to come out tonight.'

'How come?'

'Because this is Japan, Greg. It's cultural. You've been flown here all expenses paid, with Bill at your beck and call, and put up in a fancy hotel. It's only polite that you join the group for dinner at least once.'

Of course, Bill hasn't said anything. But this trick may succeed where even Disneyland has failed. He strokes his beard, ponders, then gives a slight nod.

'I suppose I could manage a couple of hours. For the sake of politeness.'

Kabukicho is near Shinjuku. It seems close to our hotel according to the map but takes half an hour on the Marunouchi subway line. The train isn't as crowded as I'd expected. There were no white-gloved subway staff pushing people into overcrowded carriages. When we arrive, neon towers above us. Multi-coloured flags with stylised kanji calligraphy hang from the buildings. The street isn't narrow per se, but the people bustling along make it appear that way. Hawkers stand in doorways, trying to get us into their establishments. One is not Japanese, and makes hand signals at Bill. But Bill brushes him off, telling him that we're going to eat noodles. We look around, wondering who is or isn't a Yakuza.

The waiters in the noodle bar look like they are dressed for martial arts training. They wear loose-fitting clothing and headbands to soak up the sweat. They yell the usual welcomes as we enter and lead us to a table at the window. Bill orders for us in Japanese; Tonkotsu ramen, dumplings and small rice dishes with fish eggs on top.

'The noodles in this place are so good, just wait and see.' After the food arrives, the French guys click their chopsticks together in a "cheers" motion. Then one of them stabs their sticks into a bowl of rice, so that they stand upright. Bill winces.

'Don't do that in Japan, guys. It's bad luck. It's similar to part of the Japanese funeral ceremony, so it's like inviting death.'

The French guys toast with Sapporo beer instead. I'm drinking green tea, Greg has a bottled mineral water, as he's on his competitor's diet again. He also doesn't eat any of the Japanese food that Bill has ordered.

'Sorry, I can't risk getting sick before the final. You know how people can need time to adjust to foreign food.'

'Don't sweat it,' says Bill.

'I saw a McDonald's up the road, I'll grab a burger on the way back.'

If Bill is upset, he doesn't show it. But I'm embarrassed at Greg's behaviour. It looks as if he'll get through this trip without attempting a single Japanese dish.

'No problem. Noodles are quick, we'll be in and out in no time. We'll swing by McDonald's as soon as we're done.' Greg seems content with this plan.

Halfway through the meal, Bill's phone rings. He gets up to answer the smallest mobile phone I've ever seen, with a flip mouthpiece. It's like something from the future. When he hangs up, Bill looks flustered.

'I'm sorry, guys, I'm going to have to run out on you.'

GREGOR: A few of us have Big Macs because we're not keen on Japanese food. Afterwards, we go to this bit a few blocks away. There's still some neon lights, but the it's also very dark. It reminds me of a scene out of *Blade Runner*. There're dozens of these wee alleyways and lanes, all connected together. The doors look like house doors. Front doors. Inside each door is a minuscule bar with only three or four seats. Loads of them are empty, some have one or two guys inside. There're no girls in these pubs, apart from the ones behind the bar, and "girl" is being generous, because they're all old enough to be my granny. It's all a bit mental for me, and I wish I was back in the hotel.

'Okay, so you guys can hang out here for a bit if you want. You could go to one of the games centres we passed on the way down, do karaoke, or, if you're over twenty, you could go have a drink somewhere. Experience Tokyo on your own without me.' I try hard not to roll my eyes, but Bill carries on: 'Here's the entrance to the subway, you take the Marunouchi line back to the hotel, the same one we used to get here. If you wander too far or you get lost, you can do one of two things. Number one, you can find a payphone and call me on my cell. Number two, you can jump into the nearest cab and show the driver this.' Bill hands out Hotel Okura business cards with his cell phone number, takes out a roll of crisp 10,000 yen notes and puts one in each person's hand. 'That's about a hundred bucks, so you have enough for a cab back to the hotel should you need it.' He does a double finger point: 'My boss is in one of these bars and wants to talk about baseball. Sometimes, I think the only reason he hired me is to talk about baseball, but he's the boss. This is one of your last nights in Tokyo. *Let loose a little.*'

We once went on a school trip to York. Mr Sivright, the history teacher, brought us to an aquarium and then slipped off to the pub. This is *exactly* like that.

Everyone goes off in different directions. The Americans ask if we want to join them. J and I say 'yes/no' at the same time, so they shrug and head off without us. J's raging at me.

'Come on, Greg. This is the first time we've been let loose!'

'I'd rather get a taxi back to the hotel. Fit some extra practice in before tomorrow.'

'You're joking? We're in Tokyo, Greg. Tokyo, Japan!'

'The finals start in less than twenty-four hours. I still have time to get better.'

'Greg. You're going to win this competition hands down. You've been playing that game for months while the others will be playing it for the *first time* tomorrow. We don't have to stay out all night, but we can't go yet. We're only here for a couple more days, this could be our last chance to hang out in Tokyo.'

'Fine. One hour. Then I'm going back.'

The micro-pub is dark, with one of those lights that make your teeth go neon blue. The pub's smaller than our lavvy in the Okura. The granny barmaid doesn't seem keen on us, saying something long in Japanese that we don't understand. We look at each other then back at her and she simplifies for us:

'Bee-ru?'

'Hai, arigato,' says J in his best Ninja voice. I hold up my hands and shake my head. I can't see in the fridge, so I ask, slowly:

'Do you have Irn Bru?'

'Eye-lon-bloo?' She spells out the name of our national soft drink. A tangy orange fizz that outsells Coke in the homeland.

'Irn Bru is Scotland drink.'

'Wee-skee?' she says. I shake my head.

'Irn Bru no wee-skee. Irn Bru soft drink. Like Coke.'

'Ko-ra?'

'Jesus Christ, there was an arcade near the restaurant. Let's get in there for a while and spend our money on something useful.' I could be imagining things, but on our way out, I'm sure I see granny open a can of Irn Bru and take a massive slurp.

J lags behind in a huff. I can't be arsed with him when he's like this. He knows what tomorrow means to me. I shouldn't be out here mucking about. I should be practising.

Near the arcade, a sleeveless foreign guy approaches us. 'You want girls? Sexy Japanese girls?' I can't tell where he comes from, but I wouldn't want to get on the wrong side of him.

'We're playing video games,' says J.

'You know where to come if you want hot girls, yes?' *Jesus.*

Bill's only taken us to the red light district. The foreign guy then tries to push me into the door of his club. Not backwards at coming forwards, are they?

'My friend's already told you we're going to the games centre,' I say, looking him right in the eyes.

'Forget games. Get real action. Japanese, Russian, Filipina, Korean? What girls you like, bro?'

'I'm not your bro,' I say, glowering. He's bigger than me, but my beard makes me look older and I'm just as wide as he is. He smiles and backs off, but the night goes from bad to worse.

'Let's get inside, Greg,' says J, putting a hand on my shoulder. I shrug it off.

'Stop telling me what to do. You're not my mother.'

'What's with the attitude?'

JUNAID: 'This guy's a dickbag. That's what's with the attitude.' Greg throws his hands in the air. 'Jesus Christ. I'm going back to the hotel. This is bollocks, and I should be practising.' He starts to walk up towards the main street, but I don't move. After a few metres, he turns.

'J. Are you coming?'

'No.' He takes a few paces back towards me, and the pimp seems to think we're talking about going into his brothel. He's back in between us, arms on our shoulders, ushering us towards the door.

'My main men. Ready for action now, huh?'

I wish the situation involved me saving some damsel in distress. The truth is that my mouth just can't hold it in.

'What's your problem, Greg?'

'I want to be left alone. That's my problem. I've got a competition to win. It's important. I shouldn't have bothered bringing you here. I should've done this on my own.'

'If all you wanted to do was come here and sit in a hotel

playing a game that nobody gives a crap about, then yes, d'you know what? You should've come on your own. It's about time you grew up.' It's clear to the pimp that we're having a proper barney now, and he leaves us to it.

'That's rich! What about you? You've been following Daize and me about like a sheep for years. If anybody needs to grow up, J, it's you. You're a coward. Piss off and grow yourself a pair.'

'"Daize and me"? There is no Daize and you, she's been in Australia for months.'

'And whose fault is that? I saw you in bed at the B&B, I'm not an idiot, J, you've been after her since she had her operation.'

'Are you listening to yourself? Does that make you feel better? Pulling excuses out of your arse to explain why you got dumped?'

'If you know what's good for you, you'll shut your mouth!'

'D'you know what? I did sleep with her. Is that what you want to hear? We came back to the B&B, and we were at it all night. With you in the next room. All so that you'd still be crying about it a year later.'

I'm on the ground. Greg's hit me. It was a good one. I jump back up and dive into a grapple. He kicks at my shins and lifts his knees into my groin, I headbutt and try to turn him around as he pulls at my hair.

'What do you know about it, dickbag? You don't know anything!' He takes handfuls of my t-shirt, tries a headbutt of his own. 'She's my…She was my…' Then Greg does something right out of my reality self-defence classes. He bites me. Clamps his jaws around my upper arm and tries to rip my bicep off.

I jerk back and fall over. His teeth have pierced the skin, the red marks will be a mouth-shaped bruise in the morning.

A few tears of blood roll down my arm. Greg paces like a caged beast, mumbling and grinding his jaw. I get up.

'Come on then. Hit me.' Greg frowns, raises his fist. I say it again. 'Hit me!' He shakes his head.

'You're not worth it.' He drops his fist, starts to walk away.

'Who's the coward now, Greg?'

TRACK 14: THE BLOOD

GREGOR: I come into the hotel room and go mental. First, I sweep everything off the coffee table, but it's not much. I pick up a book and throw it at the TV, but it misses and hits the wall behind it. I throw a magazine next, but the pages flutter out and slow it down, and it lands flat on the end of my bed. The TV. I could chuck it out the window. I pick it up, but feel stupid. Plus, if I trash the hotel room, then there goes my place in the competition.

The Irata PKD winks at me.

'Right.' I stamp on it. It's J's head, and I stamp it into the floor. Stamp the arrogant, self-centred, backstabbing dickbag right into the ground. How could he say that to me? After all the times– after everything! The casing of the PKD cracks and the insides break and fall out. Now little more than a stringy mess of wires and broken plastic, I pick it up and hurl it into the bathroom. Worthless. A grand's worth of equipment wrecked, and I don't feel any better.

Daisy was right. I never wanted to go to Australia. I tried to get into the idea, to want to do it. But that was more for her benefit than mine. I thought that by the time we finished school, she'd change her mind, 'cause she changes her mind about stuff every week. I just thought things would keep going like before, like always. Nothing was wrong with our lives. Why change anything?

It's all change, though, isn't it? Change or be dumped. Change or be cheated on. Change or die. And for us lot that don't want to change? Who were fine how we were before everyone went mental? We don't matter to anybody, apparently. We get caught up in everyone else's selfish BS. I try to think about other things, but I keep coming back to him and Daisy in that hotel bed. That's when I remember that I have it.

I get the engagement ring and open the window as far as it'll go. I take the ring from the box, and I sling it out into the dark.

JUNAID: In the closest alley I can find, I leave a violent deposit of tonkotsu ramen on the wall. The vomit splashes onto my jeans and trainers. I wipe my mouth on the back of my hand.

After Greg stormed off, I went straight back to the micro-bars and spent Bill's 10,000 Yen on the cheapest sake they had. Three small jugs later, I don't know my arse from my elbow. I go in circles around Shinjuku, hoping to stumble upon the famous love hotels. Disney castles with S&M dungeons are in the streets around me, and I need a bed to sleep it off in. Or maybe I could find one of those capsule hotels for salarymen who miss the last train home. I walk around. It could be for minutes or it could be for hours. I get funny stares from *gaijin*–foreigners–and Japanese alike. They can all–

I throw up again.

I'd best go back to the Okura and get my own room, hide out until the competition's over. It took half an hour in the subway to get here from the hotel, so I'm pretty sure I can walk back. I set off in the direction I guess to be south.

Time passes differently when you're drunk. It spins and slows down, becomes bendy and long. Underwater sluggishness. I hate that one. I walk through streets that begin to look the same. Motorways snake into the sky, the tentacles of a hungry leviathan. I piss on one of the stilts holding up a tentacle. I eat and drink from glowing vending machines. When I get to the point that I can't struggle on much further, I'm right outside an appropriate place to stop.

A graveyard.

I doubt the Okura gives out rooms to drunken tourists who walk in off the street. I need to sit down, get my head together and sober up. This is the perfect place. It's big and dark and has lots of black corners to rest in peace. I go through the gate and make my way around the edge. A map says, "Aoyama Cemetery" and labels the plots with numbers. In the dark centre, I pick a tomb, lay down and pass out.

It's the tent again. Before Guide-babes graced the Campull with their freckled faces and sticky fingers. My tent was pitched in our strip of the shared back garden. Skud was in there with me. Even now, I have no idea where he got the nickname. We'd been reading comics, eating chocolate. I was scared to be his friend, but more scared not to be. The sun turned the inside of the tent a bright orange. The shadow of the poles bent across his body. He looked out of the tent door, then pulled the zips closed.

I didn't know what I thought was going to happen, but I remember closing my eyes, embraced for a pain that didn't come. I thought it was something you did on your own, but we were doing it together. Like our heartbeats, it got faster and faster. It didn't feel like much of anything at first, but then it felt like *everything*. We clamped our mouths shut when the shudders came, trying to be quiet. There could have been a neighbour hanging out their washing. We held our breaths for a moment, and, when it became clear that we were alone, we burst into giggles.

We lay back in the tent and stared at its roof. I felt as though there was no one else in the world but us.

Before he left, Skud swore me to secrecy.

'You have to promise me,' he said.

'I promise.'

'I mean it, Jun. Never tell anyone.'

DAISY: Chris takes long strides, keen to get out into the water. To see what I've got. I stand on the shore and look for a minute, taking it in. For the first time since I arrived, it actually feels like I'm in Australia. The rest of the world's where I left it. I breathe in the ocean air; it cleans my insides. The sand is hot beneath my feet, the sun warm on my skin. I smile.

It probably goes without saying that the Coral Sea of the South Pacific Ocean is different from the North Sea off the Scottish coast. For one thing, I'm definitely not in a wetsuit. I'm wearing my rashie and boardies, newly acquired from Kelly's surf shop, my eighteenth birthday present to myself. The water hits me different as I step in. It's softer than at home. My breath catches as I'm overwhelmed by the moment, but I come back to Earth by dunking my head under and wetting my hair.

'Daisy Parker. You all right?'

'Fine. Never been in without a wetsuit on.'

'This is how it's supposed to be,' says Chris. Waist deep in the water, she holds the nose of my board as I get into position on top of it. The beginner's board is thick and wide and orange and hideous. More like a life raft than a surfboard. Chris holds me in position as I lay on the board, waiting for a wave. I try to focus on the ocean taking its breaths below me. How alive it feels. But mostly, I'm crapping myself. Broken waves lift me up and down. Chris gives a sparkly smile.

'Remember to paddle. One. Two. Three. Then up.' This must be so boring for her, waiting to push this beginner onto a small, easy wave, but she doesn't show it. She's patient and seems as excited as I am. I listen carefully. It's been a long time since I knew this stuff.

'Exactly like we did on the beach, right? You can come up to your knees first until you get the hang of it, or go; plank, back foot, front foot, then stand up tall.' I nod. Concentrating and a bit wobbly, despite the sturdy board. A wee wave comes along, and I'm convinced I'll nip right up onto it. I paddle, paddle, paddle jump, landing bang into a stance. The board flies forward as I go back, my arse sticking out too far. I'm flicked off and dunked into the blue, getting a nose full of salt-water for my efforts. I taste it in the back of my throat. When I get back above the surface, Chris is next to me.

'You all right?'

I'm grinning like a numpty.

'I did it!'

'Nearly,' she says. 'But your arse was sticking out too far.'

I nod. 'Okay.'

'It feels weird, but you need to look up, not down. You need to stand up, be tall.'

A few more tries and I can make it to my knees. I ride one wave right into the shore, putting my left leg up, but not quite getting onto both. She follows me in and gives me a pep talk.

'Here's the interesting part about learning how to surf. You need to do things that contradict human nature. No matter how counterintuitive it is, you have to push through that. It doesn't feel at all natural in the beginning, but trust me, it'll be worth it.'

'Okay.'

'So. What are the sides of the board called?'

'The rails.'

'Good job. And, as humans, our natural instinct is to grab

on when things get a little scary. But in surfing, it's the opposite. Show me where your hands should be on the board.' I lie on the board and put my hands either side of my chest. She nods. 'Exactly. But you're not doing that.' She takes fistfuls of sand and holds them in front of me. 'You're like this, grabbing onto the rails.' She opens her hands to let the sand drop. 'You gotta let go of the rails, Daisy Parker.'

Back in the water, I don't bother transitioning onto my knees. I jump right up and sail along the wave, water chattering at the front of my board. I'm a bit unsteady for a couple of seconds, readjust, and then start to flow with the wave. It's a tiddly one, but it still courses behind me, driving me forward, propelling me faster and faster. When I know that I'm standing up and steady, I get cocky and try to turn. My board does the usual flick, and I plummet into the sea. The sound of the world disappears from my ears, and I open my eyes. My board tugs on the strap that connects it to my ankle. Blue-green haziness all around. Heaven. I scream an ecstatic scream under the water. *How'd you like that one, old man?*

The sound rushes into my ears when I get back above the surface. When I turn around, Chris is further away than I expected. She raises her arms above her head as if I've won the world championships, and she whoops at the top of her voice.

'Yeah, Daisy Parker! *That's* how you get on your feet!'

I can't take the smile off my face.

TRACK 15: A NIGHT LIKE THIS

GREGOR: It happened at the school disco. What a mental night. There was a drugs raid, and half the football team were busted. Skud died that night; something that messed J up for ages. This was four years ago, parts of it still feel close, but others don't seem real now.

I remember getting into a stupid fight that night. I'd point blank refused to go to the disco with Louise Cowe, and she spouted some lies to her brother about me coming on to her or something. Dickbags, the pair of them. Louise and I had snogged once (and only once). But I remember telling J that we'd done more than we had, trying to impress him. It was all so stupid, but that fight led to Daisy.

'Ho, ho, ho. What do we have here?' said Louise's brother. "Cowie" we used to call him, or the "Tango Man", because he was forever using his mam's sunbed.

'Who are you supposed to be? Santa?'

'Piss off, Buchan. You know what this is about.'

'It's not true.'

'Not what Louise says.'

'No offence, Cowie, but we all know about your sister. Ask

your pals, they've gone further with her than I have.' One of his football chums cracked up at that, Cowie turned around and told him to shut it.

'Think you're funny, Buchan?'

'Not as funny as your fake tan.' His mates made hacking sounds in the back of their throats trying to hold in laughs. Cowie's face went even more orange. I was about as scared of Tango Man Cowie as I was a box of kittens. When he started to prattle on again, I slapped him. Problem was, his mates got involved after that. They didn't all join in at once (thankfully), maybe because J was there as well. I know I got a couple of good punches in, because Cowie's face was a mess at school the following week. But I don't remember much, because I fell and cracked my skull on the concrete. It's a blur after that. When I came back to my senses, there were adults on the go, Miss Duncan from English and Mr Robertson the P.E. teacher. Cowie and his mates had bolted, and Miss Duncan was shouting at them to come back.

A few years on, it's difficult to give the specifics. I don't remember much about the fight or the drugs bust. But I'll tell you something I remember like it was yesterday; Daisy's outfit. Every inch of it. She was dressed like something out of *Beetlejuice*. Doc Martens and fishnets, a wee tartan skirt so short that you could see the stockingy bit at the top of her tights. She had a black vest top and fingerless gloves that went right up over her elbows. Lips, nails and eyes were black. Her hair was black and sticking out in all directions with a streak of white in it as if she'd been struck by lightning. Always black, for the longest time. I didn't feel love at first sight, not the Disney kind anyway. But I was fascinated. Who was this person and why was she in a room behind the sports hall at a crap school disco?

We got separated from J while the police search went on.

Daisy took my hand, smiling when I looked at her. She made me nervous.

'D'you want to go for a walk when we get out of here?' I don't know where that came from, but I wasn't ready to leave Daisy yet. My parents thought I was staying at J's house. This meant I was free to stay with this girl all night if I wanted to. It didn't matter where we went, as long as I could be with her.

'Okay.'

I pulled J aside after we'd all been searched and were waiting for lifts home. He told me I was being stupid. I couldn't stay out all night; it was November, it was freezing, how would I get back to Cairn Bay? None of that mattered when I found myself falling in non-Disney fascination-love with the cute goth in the short skirt.

'Cairn Bay is less than five miles away,' I told him. 'I'll walk.'

Daisy and I walked along the esplanade down at the beach. I knew the reason most couples went down there and I was shitting myself. Daisy didn't speak as much as I did, but she smiled a lot. She never opened her mouth when she smiled, embarrassed of her braces. I babbled on about anything that came into my head. Video games mostly. I told her I'd teach her how to play *Street Fighter*, that I liked the way she looked in her outfit. She stepped out in front of me and looked me in the eyes. We kissed at the end of the promenade for ages.

Before Daize, I'd only snogged Louise Cowe (and only once), but I still knew this was special. Natural. I remember being scared that it was some kind of dare, that she'd turn around and laugh at me at any second. But she didn't. She bit and sucked at my neck, leaving an almighty bruise that took weeks to fade. My folks and my brothers gave me hell for the love bite, but I wore it with pride.

'Want to come back to mine?' she said.

'What about your mam and dad?'

'It's just me and my mam.'

'Oh.'

'Don't worry about her, she'll be too out of her face to notice anything.'

'Okay.'

Daize stayed in a newer area of Invergowan. Small and medium-sized houses for newlywed couples starting married life. Daisy's had three bedrooms. One bedroom was downstairs at the back of the house, along with the living room, kitchen and bathroom. Two bigger bedrooms were upstairs. The night of the disco, the whole house was in darkness.

'Daisy, is that you?' Daisy put a finger to her lips, then whispered.

'Go upstairs. Room on the left-hand side. I'll be up in a minute.'

I pointed at my feet and shrugged, trying to ask if I should take off my shoes. Daisy found this hilarious, covering her mouth with both hands to hold in a giggle. That got me started, then I was keeping my laughs in as well. I've no idea why this was so funny, but I remember that, clear as a bell. The first of many laughs we couldn't keep under control. I'd a good feeling about her, about what might happen between us. She shook her head, telling me to keep my shoes on, pointed up the stairs and turned her back on me. If she looked at my face, she was in fits of giggles.

When she went to deal with her mam, I snuck halfway up the stairs and listened. It wasn't pretty. I heard the sound of throwing up, the clunk of glass and I could smell the living room from where I stood on the stairs. The stench of drink was overpowering, like her mam'd been sweating out alcohol. She must've been in some state. I heard them clunking about, and then:

'No, no, NO!'

Something smashed, and I bolted right in there. The smell of booze hit my nose and throat; smoke nipped at my eyes. It was horrible. The thick curtains kept the room in near-blackout. A few candles gave the place dim light, the wax already liquid in their wee metal containers. The dark of the room made a framed picture of Daisy look like she had black holes for eyes.

Her out-of-it mam was half off the sofa, Daisy trying to lift the floppy body. When Daize saw me, she was mortified. I felt guilty for coming into the room in the middle of this, but I wanted to make sure everything was okay. She'd told me to wait upstairs, but I took the other side of her mam. And then I said something that cemented whatever it was we'd felt so far, at the school and then kissing down the beach:

'Please tell me we're not taking her up the stairs.' Daisy bit her lips from the inside to hold in her laugh but couldn't help herself. She laughed so hard that she snorted. Her mam did a telepathic snort then too, and we had to drop her back on the sofa and run into the hall to let the giggles out. I decided then that Daisy was for me. Embarrassment, or maybe it was pride, disappeared. When we looked at each other from then on, it was with something like relief.

We resumed our positions on either side of her mam.

'What's your mam's name?'

'Grace.'

'Nice to meet you, Grace.'

We took her to a room at the end of the hall, the closest bed to get her into. It was Daisy's room. Plastic glow-in-the-dark stars were stuck to the roof. You couldn't see the walls for posters; Joy Division, Siouxsie and the Banshees, Echo and the Bunnymen. Robert Smith and the Cure took up more space than anybody else. Daisy's hair, apart from her streak of lightning, was just like Smith's. We dropped her mam on top of the single bed. I wondered how many times Daisy'd had to do this.

I left her to the tucking in on her own and went back to pick the smashed glass off the living room floor. I opened the window to let in some air and flushed the contents of the pukey bin down the lavvy. I blew out the few candles that were still burning and put on the main light. There was a picture of her parents' wedding day, and I noticed that Daisy was a gothed-up version of her mum. Grace is wearing a silky white dress, her hair in a bun. She stands next to a tall, wavy-haired, bushy-bearded bloke in a kilt. Daisy's mam and dad are grinning like idiots in the photo.

'His helicopter went down on the way out to the rigs. Nine of them died. Instantly, they reckon. Mam's been like this since.' I never noticed Daize coming back into the room.

'I'm sorry.'

'It's okay.'

'When was that?'

'A little over a year ago.'

'Aye. I remember it in the news. My dad and brothers work on the rigs as well. You remember stuff like that.' My dad shrugs these things off, says it happens to others, but it won't happen to him. Daize's dad was one of the "others". He was only thirty-eight when he died.

'You can go home if you want.' I wondered if this was her way of telling me to bugger off. But going home was the last thing that I wanted to do. I'd just cleaned up her mam's puke, but I'd never fancied anybody as much as I fancied Daisy Parker.

'Do I have to?'

'No.'

'Good.'

Upstairs was her mam and dad's room. Nobody went in there much at that point; her dad's clothes were still in the wardrobe. There was another room upstairs, with wall to ceiling shelves full of vinyl on the back wall.

'This was his music room.' The blue room had a window that looked out to the garden. Daisy slept in there most nights, in a nest of blankets and pillows. Next to the bed was "Scratchy" the turntable. Huge headphones with a long, curly lead went from "Scratchy" to the bed. In the opposite corner was a 1960s egg chair, covered in black clothes. 'This is where I sleep. My mam's in my room most nights.' I nodded.

'How many records?'

'Almost three thousand.'

'Got a favourite?'

'I've loads of favourites. Depends.'

'Depends on what?'

'Mood.'

'What's your mood now?'

'Do you know the Beach Boys?'

'The guys that sing "Surfin U.S.A."?'

'Aye. But that's not their best album.' I thought *Surfin U.S.A.* was a song, I didn't know it was an album. 'I'll play you the best one.' She unplugged the headphones and put on *Pet Sounds*. We got into the nest and lay down to listen. She snuggled into me, humming along with the songs. I stroked the white streak in her black hair and kissed her if she looked up at me. The last song I heard before I fell asleep was 'God Only Knows'.

KISS ME, KISS ME, KISS ME

TRACK 16: CATCH

JUNAID: My mouth tastes as if somebody's shat in it. A marching band already throbbing grey in my skull. Last night comes flooding back, filling my ears with blood and embarrassment. I leave the cemetery and walk until I find a vending machine. In Tokyo, this never seems to take more than a few minutes. I need water, but I'm not paying attention and get a bottle of "Pocari Sweat" by accident. *Great*. I've heard about Japanese vending machines, and fear that there is actual sweat in this bottle. I rinse out my mouth, gargling and spitting into the nearby bin. Turns out Pocari Sweat is an energy drink; sweat replacement. It tastes like life. I get another and down it. It's infinitely better than the hot, burny, paint-stripper that got me into this state in the first place. I grab a third bottle for later and head back towards the cemetery.

The graveyard has the same "alive" feeling of graveyards back home. The difference is that it's mostly tombs and columns, with the occasional headstone. Back home it's the opposite, gravestones with the occasional column or tomb. Sticks as tall as I am stand near many of the graves. Kanji burned into them, like giant incense ready to be set alight.

Tributes? Or mystic spells for carrying people over to the other side?

A black crow stands on the edge of a bin, dipping his beak in and out. He turns to face me, checking me over for food. He's massive, over a foot tall and with piercing, milky eyes. His head jerks as he flicks it from side to side, then he takes flight, opening his wings and aiming for the trees. His wing-span must be three feet from tip to tip. Do crows get that big or am I still drunk? Maybe he's an indigenous Japanese bird, bred to attack gaijin. Or perhaps he's an Irata robot, spying on the stray sidekick from the *Temple Warrior* group. Bird noises start up in the trees; cool, smooth haikus of loneliness.

Leaves whisper from the ends of branches. If it weren't for the skyscrapers towering in the distance, I wouldn't know I was in Tokyo. That and the unusual graves. There's a giant headstone, at least twice my height, covered in elaborate inscription. There's also a three-foot marble egg, as well as tombs with model pagodas, shrine gates and monk statuettes. I'm alone, but feel surrounded.

I drink more Pocari Sweat.

Turning into another row, I come across a stone written in English. It must be the only one in the entire cemetery. The writing's faded and parts are worn away, but I can read the whole inscription:

IN LOVING MEMORY
OF
WILLIAM HENRY STONE
BORN AT SLIGO, IRELAND. 18TH JUNE. 1837.
ENTERED INTO REST
AT TOKYO THE 3RD JUNE. 1917.
DEEPLY MOURNED
FOR FORTY-FIVE YEARS A LOYAL AND
HONOURED SERVANT OF HIS IMPERIAL

JAPANESE MAJESTY'S
GOVERNMENT.
REST IN PEACE.

I think about Skud. About what he said in the tent. The last words he ever said to me.

The same crow from earlier lands on the tombstone, dancing from foot to foot and finding my eyes. We both tilt our heads at an angle to look at each other. He bobs his head forward as he lets out a low, even call towards the trees behind us. Another crow replies, and my crow takes off to find it. I don't know why, but I think of a story we were told on the self-defence course:

One day, a young and an old monk were walking along a road that had been left muddy and full of puddles by the rain. A woman needed to cross but didn't want to get her expensive clothes dirty. She scolded her servants for having too many packages to carry her. The older monk picked the woman up and trudged through the mud to get her across without ruining her dress. After he put her down, the woman swatted the old monk to the side before screaming at her servants to hurry up.

The old monk said nothing, and he and his young companion carried on up the muddy road. When they arrived back at their temple, the young monk could hold it in no longer.

'That woman was selfish and rude, she pushed you to the side without saying thank you. Why on Earth did you carry her?'

The older monk replied:

'I put her down hours ago. Why do you carry her still?'

The class was asked to think about the things that we were still carrying, and if it was about time that we put them down.

I've been using Skud as an excuse for too long. The way

things happened with him doesn't mean that's the way things'll happen with me. His dad ended up in jail, is still there for all I know. I can't imagine how lonely Skud must have felt in his situation. But I still need to put him down, to stop carrying him.

He died, and I need to let him go.

'I forgive you,' I say out loud, though I won't allow tears to form in my eyes. 'I forgive you, I forgive you, I forgive you.'

But by then, I'm not sure who I'm talking to.

GREGOR: I wake up on the sofa. There's a nanosecond where everything's okay, but then last night comes back into my head. Japan, the competition, the fight with J. I lie to Bill, tell him that we both came back to the hotel early.

The smashed PKD is on the other side of the room.

It's the day of the championships.

The ring's gone forever.

JUNAID: In the hotel room, I find Greg's already gone to the Tokyo Video Games Show. It's the day of the championships. I order two sandwiches and discover the remains of what used to be the PKD on the bathroom floor. I get in the shower. The simple use of a toothbrush is heaven. After devouring one of the sandwiches, I brush my teeth again, scrubbing more fur from my tongue. I scrawl "good luck" on a hotel postcard and leave it on Greg's pillow. I stuff a bag with my passport, clean underwear and the other sandwich. The last thing I grab is the *Lost in Japan* guidebook I bought at the airport in London. Sometimes you have to be lost to find what you're looking for.

Getting on the Shinkansen's as easy as following the guidebook. The train is a white, aerodynamic bullet resembling a NASA space shuttle. It leaves on time. Something I'm not used to. It rockets through the train stations, leaving nothing but a thunder-rumble behind. According to the notices, we're travelling at up to 225Km/h. Droplets of rain spark the windows, which frame the might of *Fuji-San* in the distance. *Fuji-San* is the guidebook's name for Mount Fuji, Japan's highest mountain and a dormant volcano. I want to ponder its strength, its spirit, but it doesn't seem real. It's a vast shadow shrouded in fog. Instead, I think about shadows, and how they lengthen in the sun, long-bending up walls.

It takes two hours to get to Kyoto, where the rain's turned to sunlight. My guidebook has a list of Kyoto "Must-Dos". A shrine called 'Fushimi-Inari-Taisha' is number one on the list. I get a taxi straight there and am dropped off at the bottom of a hill lined with sweet shops.

The key feature of this shrine is that it's lined with ten thousand red-orange gates, called "torii". The guidebook tells me that this is all to do with the god of rice. Ten feet high and made up of two columns linked across the top, the gates are as little as twelve inches apart. Gate after gate after gate creates a tunnel all the way up the mountain. The tunnel glows with a burnt-orange hue as the sun lights up the route to the top. The potential for a spiritual experience is in the air. Unfortunately, there's a mass of tourists, snapping pictures and jabbering a hundred languages.

There are Stone foxes scattered all over the shrine, many carrying keys in their mouths. When I make it to the top, an elderly couple have a small fire burning and are on their knees at an altar. They've found the spirituality I desire. The beauty of the surroundings, and the marvel of the endless torii tunnels is affecting. But it's just too busy. On the way back down the mountain, I look out to the forest, thick and deep; a Ghibli dream. I try to sense spirits amongst the trees, samurai warriors or meditating monks. But a gaggle of spandex-clad, chatty old ladies power-walk by and bring me back to Earth.

On the path in front, a group of Italians snap pictures. Hand signals accompany every syllable they bombard at each other. One blows a puff of cigarette smoke into my path.

I need to get away from tourists.

I find a group of people queuing for dumplings and join the line, hoping to spot a reclusive geisha out for lunch. While I wait, I open *Lost in Japan* and skim through the contents. Each city has a section called "Random", so I flip to "Random Kyoto". A foot massage place in Gion back streets, a café where you can go and stroke cats and a museum full of Kaleidoscopes.

Eeny.

Meeny.

Miny.

Mo.

GREGOR: We're let loose into the madness of the Tokyo Video Game Show. All-access passes. The competition starts at 6PM, so we've still got loads of time to kill. We can't play *Temple Warrior* until two hours before it starts. The whole thing is mental. It's like ten GamesMaster conventions rolled into one. Hundreds of stalls, and people lining up for pictures with people dressed as their favourite video game characters. I watch the Russian girl have her picture taken with Mario, Luigi and Princess Peach. I might as well try some new games while I'm here and join the line to play *Tekken*.

After queuing for twenty-five minutes, I get to play a round. *Tekken* might give *Temple Warrior* a run for its money. Back in the queue to play again, I get thrown off my stride by a familiar sound:

'SSSSHOOOOORYUUUUUKENNNNN!' The scream comes from Ryu, the character I play in *Street Fighter*. This is immediately followed by a live version of the game's music on pan pipes. Then drums start up, and the music has a techno beat. Dancers punch and kick their way through a strobe light martial arts routine. A screen shows us clips from the newest addition to the *Street Fighter* franchise: *Street Fighter Alpha*. And then there she is, with her legs, and her silk and her hair up in buns. And there she is again, and again, and again, and again and again. Chun-Li. Six of them, high-kicking their boots to the roof. Isn't it funny how this happens? When you want to get something out of your head, to move beyond it and focus on getting your life back, how that exact thing follows you across the world. And multiplies by six.

JUNAID: The Kaleidoscope museum has no visitors. *YESSSS!* When I arrive, there's a girl about my age and an old lady at the reception desk. The lady is reading a manga comic covered in androgynous young boys, the girl is dusting behind her. I venture some Japanese from the guidebook:

'Ohayōgozaimasu.'

'Konnichiwa,' says the old lady, brightening up. I said, "good morning", but it's the middle of the afternoon. I correct myself.

'Ah, konnichiwa.'

'Myujiamu no naka wo goran ni naritaidesuka?' Whoa. *What was that?*

'Um, kaleidoscope museum desuka?' I'd practised that all the way here, though I knew I was in the right place.

'Haaaiiiii. Sō desu.' She punches numbers into a calculator. She shoves it under my nose: 'Go hyaku en de gozaimasu. Arigatōgozaimasu. Ikemoto-san!' The dusting-girl looks our way, and I figure that she's "Ikemoto-san", 'Tenjikai no junbi shitoitena. Sokode mattemoratteru gaijin no okyakusan daikin itadaiterusi.' My translation of the Japanese is *"escort this fine young gentleman around the museum"*. But for all I know, she called me a loser.

Whatever she said, I'm sure I heard the word "gaijin", and

am a little sad at the sound of it. She turns back and says *sumimasen* which is "sorry" or "excuse me" and then;

'Tadaima tenjikai no junbi wo shiteorimasu. Shōshō o machi itadakemasu deshōka?' And then 'arigatōgozaimasu'. There's a bow, she opens the door to the museum and then she says 'dōzo'.

Inside, the museum is teensy. I go to the first table and pick up a kaleidoscope. Holding it up, I watch the colours turn and transform into a sea of moody blues and purples. It's a good one. Hand-made. Someone took a lot of care over it. There are dozens of these dotted around, of various sizes. One looks like a telescope, another like binoculars. There is one you have to look in as if it's a microscope, turning a handle to make the colours and shapes swim around inside. Some have beads and gems; others seem as though they have jewellery in them.

'Shima-san made all of these.' My mouth hits the floor– Ikemoto-san has no Japanese accent at all. 'Shima-san is the old lady at reception.' After I process this Japanese person speaking perfect English, I manage a reply:

'I wondered if they were hand-made. Shima-san must love kaleidoscopes.'

'She does,' I get a smile. 'What's your name?'

'Junaid. But my friends call me J.'

'Nice to meet you, Junaid-san. I'm Aiko.'

'Are you American?'

'No.' She laughs, she must get that a lot. 'But my family lived in Michigan until I was eight. And I watch a lot of movies.'

'Cool.'

'How about you? Where are you from?'

'Scotland.'

'Sukottorando?' Her accent goes heavy Japanese for a second.

'I, uh, don't look or sound like most people from Scotland, I guess.'

She ignores my comment, falling back into her pitch-perfect American-English:

'We don't get many people from Scotland in the museum.'

'No?'

'This is a good one.' She hands me a medium-sized kaleidoscope, and before looking, I steal a peek at her face. It's heart-shaped, with high cheeks and full lips. She smiles. A tooth comes out of her top gum. I close an eye and aim the kaleidoscope at her. 'Cute, right?' She's in a plain blue dress with an old-fashioned collar and a pair of yellow sneakers. A funky belt pinches her petite waist. I hand back the kaleidoscope.

'Very cute.'

Shima-san starts wailing from outside the door.

'Oh, please take a seat, it's time for the main attraction of the museum.' She pulls a stool out from under the table we're at, and the lights go down. Music starts up, and the whole room turns into a giant kaleidoscope, as lights beam across the walls. The colours dance, drop, and fade. Rainbows, beads and jewellery. It lasts a few minutes. Shima-san is teary-eyed as she beholds her life's work flowing on the walls of her museum.

When it's over, I give a round of applause, and Shima-san takes a happy bow.

'Please tell her I loved the museum and that I'm very impressed she made everything herself.' Ikemoto-san says a very long Japanese sentence. Shima-san retaliates with a longer sentence in return. I nod to their rhythm as if I'm fluent, bowing my head when it seems appropriate. At this point, I'm arigatōgozaimasued to a table of arts and crafts stuff. Shima-san hands me a leaflet and says another lengthy sentence. Aiko translates:

'Shima-san is asking if you want to make your own kaleidoscope. It'll be another 500 yen.'

'Are you going to help me?'

'Sure.' She does a single nod. Shiny eyes beam a smile that doesn't reach her lips.

'Then I'll make one.'

Aiko hands me an empty tube.

'It's easy. The tubes are done. All you need to do is put stuff in the bottom, and then decorate the outside.' She points to all the things I can use to do this. I pick up a tiny trowel, holding it like a child at a Pick 'n' Mix. She nods to say that I can help myself to the treasure trove of kaleidoscope sprinkles. So I go ahead and trowel crystally-red powder into the bottom of my tube.

'Are you here on vacation?'

'Sort of, my friend won a trip to Japan, and he was allowed to bring someone with him, so he brought me.' I add gems and beads in different reds.

'No kidding? That's amazing. Did your friend not want to come along to the museum?' I keep my eyes focussed on my work, adding a few sprigs of black.

'He's in Tokyo, we had a fight, so I came here. I just arrived this morning, I don't have a hotel or anything yet.'

'I'm sorry to hear you had a fight. It's great you decided to visit Kyoto, though. What have you done so far?'

'I went to Fushimi-Inari and the bamboo grove.' I glue strips of green paper on the outside of my tube, then test it out. It needs a little more gold on the inside.

'You've been to Fushimi-Inari already? Did you enjoy it?'

'Yes. I mean, it was cool to see. I've never been to a shrine before.'

'But?'

'It's nothing. I was looking for somewhere quiet to think, and there were a lot of tourists there.'

She nods slowly, knots her eyebrows and presses her lips together.

'Mmmm. You want someplace to think over the fight with your friend.'

'Sort of. I need to think about lots of things.'

There's a long pause.

'I know a place you can stay for the night. It's basic but comfortable. If you come back at the end of my shift, I could take you there?'

'Really? Thanks. That would be a great help.' I was going to pick somewhere from the guidebook and hope for the best.

'I finish at six. If you need somewhere to spend a couple of hours, we're close to the manga museum. They have comics in English if you're interested in reading something. In fact, if you can find it, check out *Fantasy Boys*. That's what Shima-san's reading. It's a fun story.'

'Okay. I'll check it out.'

We're both smiling as we swap kaleidoscopes. She looks into mine first.

'Hey, great job!'

'It's Fushimi-Inari. Green on the outside, red on the inside.'

I hold Aiko's kaleidoscope up to the light and peer inside. I see a swirling ocean inviting me to dive in.

GREGOR: We're (finally) led into our dressing room. Each of us has a table with our name above it and a miniature flag from our country. The foreign fighters are on the left side of the room and the Japanese fighters on the right. My table is in the far corner. We take our seats and start playing.

There's a console set up for each of us, and I select my character and start tearing through the game. I'm shattered. I hardly slept at all last night, and part of me wants to put my head on the desk and sleep, but that's not an option. I lost a full night of practice after wrecking the PKD, so need to get in my two hours before the competition begins.

Bill approaches and asks about J. Without looking away from the screen, I mumble that now is not a good time. He gives me a half smile and walks off, knowing something's up but not pressing me for info. I push last night's fight out of my mind as I get into the rhythm of the game, but then the six Chun-Lis pop up, which leads to Daisy in her outfit at the *Street Fighter* competition. That makes me think of her and J ditching me in the B&B and buggering off to get drunk together before getting into the bed and–

Channel it, Greg. You need to channel it.

I take a gulp of lukewarm Red Bull. Roll out my shoulders. Angle my TV screen so that the others can't see me tearing their characters to pieces.

JUNAID: The translated manga section is at the front of the museum, so it doesn't take me long to find *Fantasy Boys*. Pulling the comic from the shelves draws reserved smiles from women at a nearby desk. When I get the manga to a reading table, I open it up and my jaw hits the floor to find what can only be described as porn. I've to pay attention to make sure that I'm getting it right. There's a bunch of teenage boys, some who want to dominate and others who want to be dominated. This guy called "Storm" flicks his long hair about and has sex with all the other characters. It's safe to say that *Fantasy Boys* changes my opinion about Shima-san. I dump the book and run into the main part of the museum. Upstairs, I discover that *Fantasy Boys* is a type of manga known as "BL" or "Boy Love". Comics full of androgynous male adolescents having "perfect" relationships. "Perfect" because, being homosexual, their female readers feel safe from these boys.

This is a real-life genre of comic book.

Dennis the Menace and Gnasher, Desperate Dan, The Bash

Street Kids, Minnie the Minx, Korky the Cat, Oor Wullie, The Broons. Nope. We definitely didn't have BL in Scotland.

I buy a few "tankobons"–collected series of comics into paperback sized books. What's left of the afternoon I spend reading a translated manga of martial arts parables. My favourite is one about a talented karate kid. He leaves his village to find a famous teacher in the mountains. When he arrives, he's given an opportunity to talk with the master:

'What do you wish from me?' says the master.

'I wish to be your student and to become the finest martial artist in the land. How long must I study?'

'Ten years at least,' says the master. The boy thinks for a moment before he answers.

'Ten years is a long time, what if I study twice as hard as all the other students?' The master doesn't wait before answering.

'Twenty years.'

'Twenty years?' The boy is puzzled. 'What if I practice day and night with all my effort?'

'Thirty years,' is the master's reply.

'I don't understand. Why, when I say that I will work harder than any student that you've ever had, do you tell me it will take even longer?' The master leans forward, looks with intent at the keen, prospective pupil.

'When one eye is fixed upon your destination, there is only one eye left with which to find the Way.'

GREGOR: I get up to stretch. I use the lavvy. I go to buy a few more cans of Red Bull. Each time I walk up and down, I watch the other players. Check what they have and haven't figured out, how the computer's scoring hits on them. I take mental notes and then practise how to fight against their weaknesses.

I try to put everything but the competition out of my mind. It's almost time. A presenter and a cameraman come into the dressing room. Bill explains that they're going to come around asking our names and the country we represent. We have to add "desu" to the end of our names, and then "jin desu" after we say which country we're from. This is how you say "I'm Greg" and "I'm Scottish" in Japanese.

We get a few minutes to practise our best Japanese accents, then do a trial run before the camera rolls. When the presenter, a pint-sized Japanese model with a squeaky voice, gets to me, I add an extra line to my script.

'Greg desu. Scotland jin desu. Going to win desu.'

JUNAID: 'How did you enjoy *Fantasy Boys*?' A coquettish smile.

'Loved it. Ordered the series.'

'Good, right?' Aiko chuckles, covering her mouth with a hand. I give her my best art-critic nod.

'Amazing character development, profound storylines, classy artwork.'

'Yeah, the artwork's wonderful.' She puts her hand on her heart and nods. 'So. Wanna see something cool?'

'Yup.'

'Great,' she points over her shoulder, 'first we need to pick up the bikes.'

'Bikes? Where are we going?'

'Target practice.'

We head east on the quiet side street of her workplace. But it isn't long before we turn onto a sprawling road with several lanes of traffic. I keep close, watching her yellow sneakers crank the pedals, and her hair floating back on the breeze. She rings her bell on a street called *Nijo Dori* and calls out 'left'. When we turn, I recognise one of the buildings. Heian Shrine is number five on the guidebook Must-Do list. I think she's going to stop here, but instead, she zooms around the corner. I get a pang of distrust. I don't know this girl, I don't know where she's taking me. Where exactly am I supposed to be spending the night? Is she bringing me to a group of Yakuza goons who want to steal my passport?

But when I catch up, she's off her bike and smiling, and I realise where she has taken me. Kyoto Budo Centre. The oldest martial arts school in the country. Nerves and distrust get replaced with serendipity, and I feel guilty for doubting her.

A giant wooden hallway is in the centre of the compound. A picture of this is in my guidebook. It's surrounded by wood and concrete buildings, big and small, and a car park. There are boulders engraved with Kanji scattered around. I wish I could read them.

'I've been coming here since I was ten years old. I'm not good, but it's a great way to relax. To clear your head.' An incredible thought passes through my mind and vocalises itself.

'Do you do karate?'

'Is there target practice in karate?'

I think about it. 'Sort of.'

'No. I practice kyūdō.'

I've no idea what kyudo is and envisage a giant board game. A Japanese Miss Scarlett killing Professor Plum with a chopstick in the Library. She raises an eyebrow. My face has given me away.

'Don't know what kyūdō is, huh?'

'Nope.'

'It's not about hitting targets. It's about movement, precision. It's an art form. Though, from time to time I do imagine my mom's face on the targets.' Aiko has us decked out in robes. Other practitioners bow deep to her and give me slight nods of the head. I give sheepish bows of my own, but that's okay since I've no idea what I'm doing. Before we go into the target area, she explains that the Kyudo she practices is for contemplation. Or rather, "practice for practice's sake".

Aiko doesn't talk much once we're in the dojo. She opens up a wall which reveals the targets, or *makiwara* as they're called in Japanese. And tells me that they are twenty-eight metres away. She moves me through how to draw the bow, giving me a rubber arrow that I'm not allowed to fire yet.

'Practise these movements first of all.' She leaves me to it and goes to fire some. Her first arrow flies towards the makiwara at the other side. It catches the outer rim of the target. Her breathing's calm. Before she draws a second arrow, she licks her lips and rolls her neck. Then she's focussed again, and the arrow drives in deep, an inch from the centre. Three men practise on the other targets. Two of them are lucky to get the arrows halfway up the grass between them and the makiwara. The other guy seems proud to hit the bank near his target, managing to get his arrow to cover the full twenty-eight metres. Aiko's being modest about her skill level, and, putting these men to shame, appears to be in her element.

'Wanna try?'

'Definitely.' In my mind, the arrow has nowhere else to go but the centre of the target. I plan on splitting Aiko's arrow in two as I nail a perfect hit on my first attempt. The string hits my face, the arrow flies askew, and it lands halfway up the grass, two targets down from my own.

'Bullseye. That's exactly where I was aiming.' She calls out 'sumimasen' to the guy two targets down. He says 'Daijōbu, sensei.'

'Sensei?'

'You should stick to this for now.' She leads me to a makiwara that's so close it would be impossible to miss. 'Go through the moves I showed you here.' She says Japanese words as she places her feet, moves her body, gets her bow set up, raises, draws, and fires. There are about a million steps to this, and I'm doing two: pull-back-string and let-string-go. It feels good to whack the arrows into the close target though. I turn to see if she's looking, but she's off giving pointers to the men down the line. They talk to their sensei with the utmost respect. A sensei who wears yellow sneakers, works in a kaleidoscope museum and who made me read manga porn.

The last person to leave the dojo, calls back; 'Ikemoto sensei ha dōjō wo rokku shimasu ka?'

'Haiiii, daijōbu desu.' She pours me a hot tea. I notice a vending machine with Pocari Sweat.

'What are they saying?'

'They asked me if I'm gonna lock up.'

'If you're going to lock *me* up?'

'That's exactly what I'm gonna do.'

'Eh?'

'You can sleep here. There are mats, and I can bring you some blankets. You won't have to pay for a hotel.'

'Are you sure?' She nods. 'Thanks. I always wanted to spend the night in my dojo when I was a kid.'

'Hmmm? You practise something?'

'Karate, but not for a long time. I'm supposed to be a black belt, but I don't deserve to wear any belt these days.'

'You didn't say anything.'

'I'm no great master, like you, *sensei*.'

'I'm not a master of anything. I'm lucky. I could always hit the targets. My teacher says this means my mind is clear and focussed. I suppose he's right. I only miss if I'm stressed out.'

'What makes you stressed?'

'Same as anyone. Like if someone stole my newest copy of *Fantasy Boys*.'

We grab dumplings and rice balls from a 7-Eleven. She buys sweet tea, and I get a litre-and-a-half bottle of Pocari Sweat.

We leave the wall of the dojo open and listen to the sounds of the night. Everything feels far away, though I know I'll have to face it soon. But for this one night, I want to feel like everything else is far away. It occurs to me that this is how Daisy must have felt in Glasgow. I tell Aiko about Greg and the competition. I mention Daisy, but not the finer details. Then I remember the mangas I bought at the museum. Her eyes light up as she picks one out from the small pile.

'You bought this?'

'I liked the cover.'

'This is my favourite book of all time!'

GREGOR: Bill says that it's now or never for using the toilet one last time. I splash water on my face and put in eye drops. I wash and dry my hands. Stretch out my fingers. When I get back to the dressing room, Bill and the other competitors are standing up, waiting to go out on the stage. He nods at me.

'It's time.'

AIKO: I can't wait to show Junaid-san what he's bought. It was my favourite book growing up; my mom used to get me a copy every Christmas. It seems perfect for him too, considering what he's told me about his situation.

'This is your favourite book of all time?'

'Yeah. Let's read it. I'll translate for you.'

'Okay. What's it called?'

'Um. *The Light Beyond*. Something like that.'

'*The Light Beyond*. I like it.'

I sit cross-legged next to him, so we can both see the pictures. I open to the first page, and in the very first sentence is a word I don't know in English.

'What do you call those bugs that live in the bottom of ponds and swamps? The little ones?'

'I don't know. Grubs?'

'All right. So, once there was a grub. This is him here. He's called Dō. And he hates being a grub. Hiding from predators, struggling to catch food. Most of the time, he doesn't move, he just sits there waiting for food to pass by.'

'He looks bored.'

'Yeah. It is boring. But look. One day he decided to try something different. Dō decided he'd learn how to swim. Here he is copying the frogs and the fish and the snakes. But he wasn't very good until one day, he did one of these...' I put my hands on my mouth and blow a fart noise; it makes Junaid-san laugh. 'Dō went zooming through the water. And that's how he discovered he had those holes that fish use for breathing.'

'Gills?'

'Right! Gills. I should've known that one. I love the Discovery Channel.'

'He had gills in his arse? I mean, in his bum?'

'Right. In his butt. And here he is practising every day because swimming was the closest to flying he could get. He didn't have wings, he couldn't breathe real air, so swimming *was* flying. It was freedom.'

'Wait, how come he's getting bigger in the pictures?'

'Aha! We're almost at the best bit. Look. After lots and lots of swimming practice, Dō becomes the best swimmer in the swamp, or so he thinks. Because one day, another grub flies by, swimming faster than Dō ever had. He swims after her, but when he catches up and asks the secret of her speed, she says that she doesn't have time to teach him. She's leaving the swamp, and once you leave, you can never return.'

'Why?' asks Junaid-san.

'That's exactly what Dō asked. And she said to him, "in breaking through to the other side, we have to leave certain things behind." Dō was in awe of this majestic creature, the biggest of his kind he'd ever seen. He watched as she moved beyond the surface to the other side. Dō had spent so much time worrying about how hard it would be to break the surface. He now knew that it was as easy as taking a single step. He saw a dark shape drop away, and from it came something colourful. He strained against the surface, as close as he could go without breaking it. The colour lifted and disappeared.

'Dō knew that he had to do the same. He had to find out what lay above the water, even if it meant losing his life, and he began to push his head through. Now…look.'

I turn the page and reveal the great secret to Junaid-san. The second half of the manga is nothing but empty boxes. The idea is that children who get this book will create their own world above the water. Junaid-san doesn't understand. He wants a resolution, which is an adult thing. Children grab the crayons and relish finishing the story in their own way.

'But, there's nothing there. Is it a mistake?'

'No. The book is supposed to be like this.'

'But, you can't start a story and not finish it.'

'Why not? The world is full of unfinished stories.'

'But…what happens after he breaks the surface? How do I know the ending?'

'That's the whole point, Junaid-san. You write it.'

TRACK 17: THE KISS

DAISY: It's hard to keep up with people from back home. First, it's weekly, then fortnightly, before turning into a monthly affair. Those initial long letters, like the boards I use to surf, get shorter and thinner. They turn into postcards with little more than greetings, scribbles of weather, or false, wish-you-were-here sentiments. I don't wish anybody was here and I'm doing more than well on my own, thank you very much.

At one point I went two months without speaking to my mam. She freaked out the next time I phoned, telling me that all I need to do is call and say, "I'm alive", then hang up. She can't go two months without contact when I'm on the other side of the world and "anything could be happening to me".

This is what's happening to me. Life is simpler and fuller than it's ever been.

On any given day, I'll do a shift at Kelly's, getting into the water before, after, or both. There're no essays to write, no deadlines, no exams, and no boyfriend. I live on the opposite side of town, a few streets from Chris. We cycle together to work, different routes each day, silent in the mornings and chatty at night. We eat, drink, nap, read, and socialise on the beach. The cycle home becomes a tapestry of sober rides and tipsy trips during which we share our hopes and fears. Chris studies Marine Science and wants to travel the world making underwater films. Surfing isn't forever. She got the job at Kelly's after kneeing him in the balls when he made a move on her. She still has both parents, and neither has issues with alcohol. I spill my guts in front of open skies and blinking stars that are different on this side of the planet. I tell her about Dad, Mam's drinking, about how I got the money to come over. Sharing is a kind of freedom.

Any spare minute I have, I'm in the water, and I'm quick to leave the orange life raft behind. I move from a less embarrassing "funboard" onto shorter hybrid boards that are more difficult to ride. Proper shortboards need bigger waves, which need expert timing to drop onto. After I'm used to the hybrid, I buy my very own shortboard with cash hard-earned during shifts in the cafe. I get a wee sticker made that reads, *12-09-1989,* and I name the board "Lumpy". I miss that dog more than I ever would've expected. On days with big swell, I take Lumpy out. Though I'm not ready to surf the big sets, I want to know how it feels to have a raging ocean beneath me. I go out with Chris on those days, and we chat as we wait for the sets to roll in. Then I watch her punch her board down with her powerful legs, taming wave after wave. She disappears into them, and I whoop with glee when she springs out the other side.

Even on days with little or no swell, we're in the water. One evening we take out a couple of longboards. People call them "noseriders" because you can walk right to the front of them. Chris calls this "walking the plank" and "doing the Flying Lady". At the front of her board, she spreads her arms and tilts her head back to howl at the moon. That evening, I make it to the front of my longboard. I "hang five", putting my left toes over the tip of the board, but I'm not ready to "hang ten" yet. I open my arms and throw my head back for a howl, at which point I drop into the calm black of the sea.

Our bodies soak up vitamin D in the daytime and moon rays in the evening. We hang out at the café all the time, before and after work. We share beers with regulars who tell surf stories from the golden age, exaggerated tales of the biggest waves caught off the point. We roll our eyes and make fun, but love to listen to these tall tales. Kelly's tales are the tallest. He starts to call me the "Coolangatta Princess" and tells Chris there'll be a new queen soon. Most evenings, we trundle home on our bicycles, tipsy and smiling. The bond between us grows and grows, and to use the word "friend" doesn't do Chris justice.

'You're ready for bigger waves, Daisy Parker.'

'I know. I'm just not quite ready yet.'

She laughs.

'What does that mean?'

'I'm not sure.'

Chris's smile is lit up by moonbeams. We're on a flat calm sea, on paddle boards. The moon hangs in the sky, pushing and pulling the tides, and our feelings.

'Let's do a challenge,' she says.

'Okay. What kind of challenge?'

'Let's kick down to the bottom. First person to get scared loses. Or if nobody gets scared, then the first person back up loses.'

We leave everything we don't need on the large boards. We stand up, count to three, then drop into the dark below. I know that I'll win; Chris is a wimp with stuff like this. In the dark saltwater, I'm unable to pick out anything in front but the pearly nails on my fingers. I kick down to the bottom. The water absorbs everything. There's nothing but black in all directions, infinite emptiness. I look round for Chris but can't see a thing. After sitting as long as I can in the dark, I aim skyward, push, and let my own buoyancy bring me back up. I kick when holding my breath becomes unbearable. The trip to the surface is like floating through a tear in the universe.

Chris is already there.

'Jesus, Daisy Parker. That must've been about twenty minutes you were under.'

'Shut up. Two minutes, more like.'

'I'm telling you, I've been waiting here forever,' She takes a sip out of a beer can and hands me another from her backpack.

'Maybe it's 'cause time stands still down there.' It's quiet. Chris rotates her head in a circle. When it's at the back of her shoulders, the moon picks out her elongated neck. Coolangatta Queen. Merwoman.

'You should stay here forever, university is overrated.' A month in Australia feels like a week, and before I know it, my visa will have run out. I'd thought about options for staying on, though I still wasn't sure. But with the way Chris says it, the way we look at each other afterwards, it was occurring to me more and more to stay here. We talked like that, open and easy, day and night. On the beach, at work, in the pub. We'd travelled together, she introduced me to her friends and her sister down in Brisbane. I'd even met her parents by then, who welcomed me as if I were a long-lost family member.

'I'm glad I met you, Chris. You get something in me. You're...soft.'

'Soft?' She flashes me her perfect smile.

'Aye. There's an understanding that I'm not sure I've ever had before. From anybody.' I hide my face in my palms. 'I don't know what I'm saying.' Chris moves onto my board, peels my hands from my face to look me right in the eyes. *If she kisses me right now, it won't feel weird.* We've that locked eye, change-in-atmosphere, beginning-to-lean-in moment. I freak out and move my head back.

'Sorry–' I look down, then away. I hear Chris breathing.

'Do you want to kiss me?'

'I want to. But I'm not sure I can.'

She puts a hand on my face, looks deep into my eyes.

'Let go of the rails, Daisy Parker.'

GREGOR: It's a pretty mental feeling. It's kind of like I'm outside of my body, looking at what's going on from the other side of the stage.

There's a huge crowd, much bigger than I expected. The heat off the lights and cameras is so hot that I have to take my shirt off and tie it around my waist. The t-shirt that's underneath has a picture of Ryu doing a flying kick and writing across the back of it that says, "Round One, Fight!".

I can see sweat on the foreheads of the other competitors. We come up pair by pair to fight for our right to be the *Temple Warrior* World Champion. We play on standard size TVs, but a huge cinema screen hangs above us for the audience to follow the action. The light from cinema-sized versions of our characters glows on my t-shirt.

I get a similar feeling to when I was in the *Street Fighter* championships. That thing happens to my ears again. The sound of the crowd and the music and the Japanese version of Dominick Diamond all merge into one buzz of radio static. The sound's far away, or underwater. I win, and I win, and I win, and I start to feel as tall as the version of me on the big screen above. The towering, galactic version of me that I'm in control of. The me that reacts and responds in the right way, gets the things that he works hard for. That onscreen Greg that I wish I could be in real life. And this is why I'd rather be in these make-believe worlds than anywhere else.

JUNAID: The bike ride to the bottom of the mountain is about five miles. I'm off to climb Daimonji-yama. A mountain on the eastern edge of the city, famed for the giant character DAI (大) sculpted from rocks on its side. Once a year, the giant 大 on the mountainside is set on fire as part of a festival. Aiko explained that the character means "big" or "great". I also noticed that it was the same character in "Bassai dai". Bassai dai was the form, or "kata" that I had to learn to get my black belt in karate.

It was five in the morning when I left the budo centre to find the foot of the mountain. The pathway's close to *Ginkaku-ji,* the temple of the silver pavilion. Aiko gave me exact instructions to get to where I can follow the trail all the way to the top. I'll come out onto a clearing where a small shrine sits in the centre of the 大.

I find the silver temple and follow my directions to a smaller one up the street. Sure enough, I soon arrive at the foggy foot of the mountain. The bike's ditched, but I bring its headlight to get going on the path. It's all mud and gravel crunching under my feet, and I come across a small pipe of water that I've been encouraged to taste. This is the part of the mountain where I can get fresh Daimonji mountain water. It tastes good. Cool and heavy. I use a little to wash my face and fill yesterday's empty bottle of Pocari Sweat.

It's not long before the gravel path turns into wooden steps made from cut logs. They're steep but easy to see with the beam from the headlight. I march up the mountain in the half-light while most people are still sleeping. I can only see ten feet ahead, but I trust that each step is a step closer to where I need to be. When the wooden logs turn into stone steps, I know from Aiko's description that I'm near the top. I run the rest of the way. I haven't exercised since landing in Japan, and need to get my blood pumping. I bound up two or three steps at a time, and soon come out onto the stroke that crosses through the middle of the 大. I spot the shrine in the centre point of the character.

The sky has started its long change into morning, but I still can't make out the sleeping city in the darkness and fog below. The lights I'm able to pick out are like sleepy embers in a fire that's burned through the night. I'm way up high, in a cloud, what feels like a million miles above the city. I give the shrine's bell a gentle ring, bow and clap my hands. I pray to the Big God of Fire, or whoever they burn the hillside for. In my mind, it's the Big God of Fire, and whoever she is, she feels like an excellent person to pray to.

'Dear Big God of Fire. Give me a sign. Anything.'

DAISY: It's slow and soft at first. Lips brushing, just to see what it feels like. Then it speeds up. I open my mouth, feel the warmth and roughness of her tongue against mine. Then her hands are in my hair. I search out her belly and her back. It feels good. Different from any kiss I've ever had, and I lose myself in it. Kissing in the water till my heart's fit to burst.

JUNAID: I watch the sun burn through the fog, and the city come to life at the bottom of the mountain. Kyoto's surrounded by hills. Wisps of clouds hover above waking houses. Everything looks new. Brighter.

I move further up the mountainside until I'm no longer on a part that makes up the kanji. For the first time in I don't know how long, I decide to do Bassai dai, my black belt kata. Up nearer the top of the mountain, there's a small clearing with plenty of space. It's on a slope, but it'll do. I take a slug of Pocari Mountain Juice and stand for several moments. I breathe in fresh air. Feel the ground beneath my feet, real and firm, on a mountain lifetimes old. I tell myself not to think about the moves of the kata. Do them. Let the routine do the work. Let it come out by itself.

I make a few mistakes the first run-through. It's been a while, but my body remembers. The moves are still there in my bones. I practised this kata hundreds of times before I got my black belt. Morning, noon and night for months. It doesn't take long to get through the movements. A couple of minutes at most. It feels good.

I do it again, dropping the mistakes. Letting my arms drive into sharp strikes, and my feet stamp into the earth. It's like slipping on an old gi, formed around your muscles from hours of sweat and practise. Third time lucky.

The third time, I try to let the mountain come through it. If thoughts come up, and they do, I imagine them as helium balloons and let them go. I come back to the moves, one by one.

Again.

This time I do it better than I did to get my black belt. I have a rhythm going. It's almost a dance, there's a beat to it. A life.

Again.

There's no one around, so I decide to do the *kiais* this time. The shouts that are such an integral part of the katas. Bassai dai has two kiais, and until now I've been exhaling forcefully, but it's not right. There's a kiai on a downward kick, and one on a knife-hand that finishes off the kata. Bugger it. Let's wake up this town. With my hands back in the ready position, I drop all the tensions I can find lingering in my muscles. I go through the first section of kata, the quicker and slower movements. When the rhythm leads me to the first deep kiai, I try to ring the bells in all the shrines in Kyoto:

'EEEEEEEEEE!'

It's the best way to release energy. I used to look forward to karate class for the simple pleasure of shouting. If the whole world got up and kiaied every morning, the crime rate would drop to zero.

I let out another 'EEEEEEEEEE!' on the final knife-hand of the kata. Moving into ready position, I go straight back into it. Five didn't take long. Five more. Get to ten. Wake up the mountain with kiais. I'm no longer doing the kata with my head, not thinking it. That's what took me so long to learn it in the first place: thinking. I do it with my heart.

'EEEEEEEEEE!'

DAISY: I spend the next few days thinking about that kiss, about what it means. There's a smile plastered across my face the whole time. Kelly and the gang rib me at work, asking if I've found a bloke. It feels wrong and right and forbidden and fluent, and it scares the crap out of me all at the same time. I haven't felt knots like this in my stomach since I was fourteen years old. I went to a school disco I wasn't interested in to approach a certain Mr Jarvis but left with a certain Mr Buchan instead.

'Am I ready?'

'You're ready. I've been telling you for ages that you're ready. All right?'

We're out past the point break at Snapper Rocks waiting on a massive set coming in. Monsters that'll carry us hundreds of yards.

'Don't panic. It's the same as every other time you've surfed. Don't think too hard, and trust yourself. This is your time, Daisy Parker.'

I'm invincible.

GREGOR: I run on autopilot. Months and months of playing this game, there's no way any of these other guys could stop me. I get funny looks. Maybe they know I stole a PKD and that I've had way more practice than the other players. Who cares, I pick them off one by one. This is how Albert must have felt in Glasgow. I can see what happened now. He could've beat me thirty fights to nil, but he let me win. He gave the crowd a buzz, made it a night that people would speak about later. I lose, and I lose, and I lose, but then I go back to winning. I keep calm, I smile, I shake hands with opponents after "just" beating them at the last second. The crowd laps it up.

The sound comes back into my ears as I focus on my last opponent. A Japanese kid. About fifteen years old. *Albert* 2.0. Sweat drops off him onto the floor. If the same is happening to me, I don't notice. I'm calm. I flow around anything that gets thrown at me and counter as if he's whispering exactly what he's going to do into my ears. The crowd makes noise for impressive moves and combinations of hits. I win, and I win, and I win, and my opponent drops to his haunches, his head in his hands. The Dominick Diamond equivalent spouts vigorous Japanese. Models march on stage with the cheque and trophy. My opponent gets back to his feet and shakes my hand. One model puts a plastic crown on my head, the other a purple robe over my shoulders. I'm handed the cheque and trophy amongst a flurry of camera flashes.

It's my time.

I'm invincible.

JUNAID: It's after my eighth round of the kata that I see him. A Japanese man. Standing right in front of me and paying close attention. He's wearing heavy canvas trousers and a shirt. The clothes a builder or some kind of tradesman might wear. He sees me looking.

'Mountain,' he says, pointing to a logo on the chest of his shirt. Then shows me a bag and a small trowel. He scoops earth into the bag. 'I work mountain.' I nod. He nods back. I start the kata again, and he watches, fixed and peaceful. He stands close after round nine, and as I start up my tenth Bassai dai of the day, he moves with me. *He knows it.* His kiai has a different sound to mine. It shifts the birds from the trees. When he stamps down, his feet drive into the earth, moving it at his will, and it feels as though he's shaking the whole mountain. His kata goes out into the world in all directions. I don't know how he's doing it, but I can feel it around me. When we finish, we bow at the trees in front of us, and then he turns and bows to me.

'You kata very nice.'

'Arigatōgozaimasu.'

'Ah, nihongo ga wakarimasuka?'

'Oh. Sorry. Sumimasen. I don't speak Japanese.'

'Ah. Amerika?' I shake my head and struggle to sound out:

'Su-kotto-ran-do.'

'So desuka?'

I nod. I don't bother to tell him that I don't look or sound like most Scottish people.

He points me to a part in the kata, slapping his legs. I move into the same position, and he gives me a nudge, showing me that I'm too light on my feet.

'Feet heavy. Like mountain.' I try to make my feet heavy, like the mountain. He pats my belly. 'Low cen-ta. Heavy, like kiai.' I think about the kiai, and how when you release that shout, you're rooted to the ground. Nothing can move you. I shift my weight.

'Good,' he says, 'this way. All this way.' I'm unsure what this man's job is. Earth guy, geologist, tree surgeon, firestarter. It doesn't matter. I've never seen anyone do karate like he can.

'Karate,' I say, 'how long,' and then I point to him. Echoing the way he's using English and hoping that it's not offensive.

'Ah. Shi-ju-go ye-ah. Fo-tee fi-vu ye-ah.' He holds up four and then five fingers.

'What? You,' I point at him again, 'how old?'

'I do karate. Ju-ni, twe-ru-vu ye-ah oru-du.' He hasn't understood my question, but I do the maths and count that he's around fifty-seven. I can see his age in his face now, but that's probably to do with being out in the sun for his job. His body could be confused for half that. Solid. Sinewy. Veins bursting to get out of his forearms. I nod.

'I do karate eight years.' I hold up eight fingers.

'Ah. Still baby.' He laughs. But it's right. I am still a baby. I've thirty-seven years of karate to catch up with him. Years of battling ahead. Then I remember something my teacher used to say: "the only person you ever fight is yourself".

Karate-man points down the hillside.

'You live Kyōto?'

'No. I'm on holiday.'

'Ah, horiday, horiday. You come karate. Budō cen-ta!'

Holy crap. 'I went yesterday. Um...kinō...budō centre. Eh...Kyūdō.' Man, my Japanese is crap. I spent my entire train journey to Kyoto studying the phrases in my guidebook, but all I can remember is that 'kinō' means yesterday.

'Kyūdō. Hai, kinō kyūdō ga arimashita. Kyō wa, karate desu.' He slows down his speech for me, and I understand plenty of words: *kinō* - yesterday; *kyūdō* - kyudo; *kyō* - today; karate - karate. There's karate today! I have to go. I could bring Aiko and get her to help me talk to him. She has to know him. I'm about to say her name, but he speaks first.

'Tu-nai-to. Karate. You come karate.'

'Yes. I will come. Thank you for your teaching.'

'Hai.' He bows low to me, so I make sure to bow deeper. Then he takes his bag and trowel and marches up the mountain.

Two senseis in two days.

I'm invincible.

DAISY: We look to the distance. We wait. Hope that the aftermath of a storm over the horizon three days ago will ripple its way here. That a thundering energy will come to us in waves. Waves we'll use our boards to ride, to conquer.

The sets arrive, churning in the distance like a convoy of the biggest lorries you've ever seen. My stomach flips, and then so does my heart. The waves are going to be much taller than us. Four, five feet high up the back, so Christ knows what the face will be like. Double that. Chris sees the fear in my eyes.

'You paddle, and you jump. That's all you've gotta do, you with me?' I nod, 'cause my voice doesn't come when I call on it. The waves approach. We paddle into them, let a couple roll past. 'I'm taking the next one, so I can watch you after. No backing out.' She flies off onto the wave. Watching from behind, all I can see is her tipping forward before she disappears down the face. Butterflies flap their wings in my belly, trying to pull me in the opposite direction. I watch for what seems like forever, and just when I'm sure that Chris has fallen, she's been working her way back up the wave. She shoots up into the sky, screeching and hooting for joy when she lands. It gives me the push I need, and I paddle onto the next one.

'Your turn!' Chris screams at me. I paddle and paddle, unsure if I can keep up. I don't know if it's time or not, but I jump to my feet. The board surges, building momentum along the wave's massive undulation. Before I've time to think, I drop down onto it like a tossed penny. My heart in my mouth, I push to move myself to my left, trying to outrun the beast behind. The wave forms a pipeline as it folds on top of itself and starts to close over on top of me. I scream. My voice rebounds and echoes inside the cave, my board chirruping against the water. Pushing down, I break for the light at the end of the tunnel, sailing out and raising my arms in victory. Standing tall on the board and bringing my arms down in a double fist pump.

'WOOOOO!' I turn to see if Chris has seen it, and though she's fifty feet away, she throws her arms in the air and screams:

'THAT'S SURFING, DAISY PARKER!'

It lights me on fire. And I can't wait to get to her. I tear my arms into the water to move me along, Chris is doing the same to get to me. My pulse is still racing when our boards meet, clunking into each other as she leans over for a hug.

'I did it, I went down the face, the water broke on top of me, and I was in the tube. Did you see it, Chris? Did you see?'

She smiles. My eyes must be as big as saucers.

'I saw you. Working that board like a pro. How'd it feel?'

'Like I owned the Earth. Like I could do anything. But yours was better. You flew. I saw you, Chris, you flew. Like an *actual* bird.' We whoop at the sky, at the tufty clouds high up. We kiss a congratulatory kiss, pause to look at each other, frown, then come together harder. The kiss is even more charged than our first. The water makes it slidey; hair and faces and lips wet. Our hands claw and grab at flesh that burns for them. Chris uses an arm to hold onto my board and pushes me against it. We rock with the motion of each other and the waves, and I want it to go on forever. I let go of more than the rails. I let go of everything.

TRACK 18: A THOUSAND HOURS

JUNAID: The clouds disperse into the blue. The streetlights are replaced by the morning sun, which gets hotter every minute. Kyoto bustles in pockets. There's a pocket of Chinese tourists in line for the silver temple, a pocket of grannies having a morning gossip, and a pocket of cycling students, synchronised and matching in identical uniforms. I skip the turning I took earlier and continue down the street to tour the city. I've been here less than twenty-four hours, but it feels like much longer. Weeks and months. I cycle all the way down to Gion, where the traditional shop fronts match the pictures in my guidebook. I stop to ponder a map when an insect passes by my face. Six inches long, thin as the lead in a pencil and blacker than a shadow. Its silent wings flutter as it lands in the basket on the front of my bike. I reach out to touch it, but as soon as I do, it disappears. I've no idea what it is.

I walk my bike up tourist shopping streets, stopping at a sports outlet. In my sweaty state, nothing could make life better than a fresh set of clothes. I buy shorts and t-shirt with the Hanshin Tigers baseball logo, then follow the smell of food. I eat bite-sized portions of nori-wrapped rice balls, pumpkin croquettes and broiled fish. Maybe the strangest breakfast I've ever had. I head back to the Budo Centre. When I arrive, I'm surprised to see that Aiko's already there, I thought she'd be at work for most of the day. She looks as if she's been hit by a train.

'Where've you been? It only takes an hour to climb the mountain.'

'I did some karate at the top, and then went for a cycle. You'll never guess what happened, I met this guy–'

'There's been a terrorist attack in Tokyo.'

'What?'

'They thought it was a bomb, but it was gas. Poison gas.'

'I don't understand. A bomb?'

'In Tokyo. Poison gas on the subway. It's all over the news.'

I'm quiet for a moment, then: 'Greg. I have to talk to Greg. He's okay, right?'

'I don't know.'

'Did anyone, I mean, did everyone survive?'

'I don't know.'

'I need a phone.'

'There's one in the main building. I'll help you talk to someone.'

Aiko calls the Okura in Tokyo and rapid fires Japanese down the line. I hear the faint sounds of an uncharacteristically frenzied staff member.

'Is she putting you through to our room? I'm sure he's in our room.' Aiko hands me the receiver.

'She's trying to get through.' I put the phone to my ear. It rings for a while and then I hear a voice.

'Greg, it's me.' But all I get back is a string of Japanese. Aiko takes the phone.

'What does Greg look like?'

'Shorter than me. Ginger hair. You know? Red hair. Big

beard. Cowboy boots. I don't know. He's Greg. He looks like Greg.' She talks into the receiver.

'Okay, forget that. What's the competition?'

'*Temple Warrior*. On the Irata PKD console. There's a bunch of us from different countries all staying at the hotel. A guy called Bill's looking after us. The chaperone. We never used the subway. Once. We only used it once. I'm sure Greg's in our room. Can you ask her to try again?' Aiko translates my garbled response, or I guess that's what she's doing. She turns back to the receiver before I finish.

'There are French people? Russians?'

'Yes. They're here for the competition too.'

'Bill. He's American? Speaks Japanese?'

'That's him. Is he there? Can I talk to him?' But she's back on the phone. Says things that I don't understand. Says arigatōgozaimasu. Hangs up. I look at her. Wait for good news.

'You need to go back to Tokyo. The Marunouchi line was...your friends are in hospital.'

I'm somehow on the Shinkansen.

Gas.

A type of poison.

Blink.

Someone's died.

No one can explain it.

Japanese attacking Japanese.

Blink.

Is Greg okay?

Blink.

Why did they do this?

What's happening?

Blink.

No hug.

No goodbye kiss.
A phone number on scrap paper.
A push towards the ticket barriers.
Blink.
You're on top of a mountain in Japan.
Blink.
Terrorists release poison gas on the subway.
Blink.
You're alive.
Blink.
You're dead.

.

Blink.

.

Blink.

.

Blink.

.

DISINTEGRATION

TRACK 19: DISINTEGRATION

DAISY: I'm thirteen. It's a school day.

'Up, Scoob,' says Dad. I whinge and turn around to give him my back, pulling the covers up around my ears.

'I'm not going.'

Dad grizzles his stubbly chin into my neck, which I love and hate at the same time. He stops when his lips are near my ear and whispers:

'Fuck school. We're surfing.' I don't hear these words often, and leap from the covers.

'Fuck school!'

'Sssshhh. You'll wake your mam.' It's half past four in the morning. Dad's sneaking me out before Mam gets up, which means they had a fight last night. Mam doesn't mind us surfing before or after school, or on the weekends, but I'm not to miss classes unless I'm sick. 'Hurry up, I'll be downstairs.' He's wearing his faded green board shorts and a Billabong t-shirt that's all stretched and loose. He turns around and winks at me before he leaves the room.

I peek out the curtains at the midnight blue; hazy orange streetlamps light up our cul-de-sac. It's early September.

Drinking cheap wine in tents and kissing Junaid Jarvis has tainted the whole summer. Days like this help make up for it. There's reliable surf at Invergowan beach, better than most of Scotland. Waves can get up to four feet some days, and you can get thirty yards out of them. You have to wait a while for the sets to roll in though. In the kitchen, Dad's made me toast with butter and jam. A glass of orange juice. We'll eat after, but this is good enough to get me going. He fills a thermos with sugary tea. Standing by the sink to drain his mug, he watches me get jam on my face and wipe it off with the back of my hand. He doesn't say anything. Just smiles.

As we pull away from the house in the van, he rolls down his window to let the cold air in. 'Good Vibrations' plays on the stereo. A Beach Boys single from 1966 that was shoved on their 1967 album *Smiley Smile*. Always the Beach Boys on surfing days. He smokes a roll-up, even though he's supposed to've stopped, and winks at me.

'Best album in the history of man?'

'*Pet Sounds*, the Beach Boys, 1966.' It's not my answer, it's his answer, but this exchange is my favourite in the world. After I get the answer right, he always says:

'Correct.' Having affirmed that I still know his favourite album, he turns up the volume on the compilation tape. He starts up the harmony in his best American baritone. I add the next layer of 'Good Vibrations' in the best soprano I can muster at 5 o'clock on a Thursday morning. Then we finish up with 'bop bops' and 'na na nas', me drumming on the dash and Dad drumming on the steering wheel. When the song fades out, I grin from ear to ear. He pats the stereo and nods his head.

'Classic.'

'Barbara Ann' comes on next, and we're off again, twisting and jiving in our seats.

We park at the beachfront, and Dad turns the volume down. He blows into his hands and rubs them together, excited to get into the waves.

'Okay, Scoob. Here's the plan. First, we'll put our wetsuits on.'

'Aye.'

'Then we'll get our surfboards out.'

'Aye.'

'We'll go down to the water.'

'Aye.'

'An' we'll surf like fuckin' maniacs.' I snort with laughter. We're out and in wetsuits, and he carries my board as well as his own, even though I'm more than capable. We leave a trail of footprints that's mostly heel, Dad's size elevens next to my size threes. When the sand changes from soft to hard, it's cool on the soles of our feet, our toe prints more visible. We stop ten yards from the sea, stashing the thermos and van keys under our towels. The westerly wind takes our hair across our faces. I tuck a handful behind my ear and watch Dad, his eyes closed, getting in the zone.

People think the sea's blue, but that's a myth. The sea mirrors the sky. On dark days before storms, she's an ominous grey, foreboding. Today she's green off a pale blue sky. She turns blue beyond the sandbanks, getting darker and darker til she meets the horizon, an optical illusion in the distance. It wasn't that long ago I thought the world ended there, where the sea meets the sky, a straight drop into emptiness. The swell's welcoming today. Tailor-made for our purposes. Dad smiles and kisses me on top of the head, his pre-surf meditation over.

'Ready?'

'Ready.'

Surfing the North Sea's chilly at any time of the year. One of the best bits is jumping into a freezing sea and listening to the noises we make. Sucking in breaths at the cold. It makes you feel alive though, wakes you up. I start paddling out on my board. Dad next to me, looking at the sky and the birds and grinning at me after. There's not another soul in the water or on the beach. The sea bobs us up and down, waves push for shore and break in a foamy rhythm.

'You want to go first?' I shake my head. I always let Dad go first. 'Okee dokee.'

He paddle, paddle, paddle, jumps, flying off on the wave, free as the gulls in the sky. He surfs the length of it, nothing fancy, simply enjoying himself. He slopes off at the end and drops back down onto his board. Though there's swell and wind, the waves are tame. It's easy to get onto them, easy to float along them, and they don't break till they get near the shore. I aim for the middle wave of the next set, usually the biggest, but it's still less than two feet high up the back. Paddle, paddle, paddle, jump and I'm up into a narrow stance. My arms outstretched, I push my weight into my front hip to ramp up my speed. I don't have to think about Mam or school or anything beyond the ride. There's me and there's the wave, and the rest of the world disappears. That's why you surf. I'm up for ten seconds or so before dropping to my knees and lying back on the board at the end of the trip. I look at the empty beach, too young to appreciate how lucky I am. But I know that this thing I'm feeling is bliss.

Back on land, we peel our wetsuits to the waist and towel ourselves down in the white September sun. We spent the morning surfing till our fingers were pruney and our bodies shivering. Meanwhile, my pals were sat in Maths and Geography classes. This makes a day surfing all the more satisfying. We hose down the suits and boards and throw them in the back of the van. When we hop inside, Dad blasts the heating till the cab warms us up and the goosebumps leave our arms. I pour the last of the tea, and he jumps out for bacon sandwiches from the café at the beachfront. Back in the cab we eat and drink while watching the ocean. My feet are up on the dash. 'Let's Go Away for Awhile' hums low and pensive on the stereo, Dad speaking in bursts about California, Hawaii, Indonesia, and South Africa. But most of the enthusiasm's aimed at Australia. The famous spots on each coast that he's read about in surfing magazines. I don't remember if he mentions Snapper Rocks or Rainbow Bay.

'Next summer, Scoob. We're doing Australia next summer. Get that mother of yours convinced to come surf with us, eh?' I look at him, nodding along. I know the stories of the people who started surfing here in the old days. They made their own boards out of foam and fibreglass in the garages their pals worked in as mechanics. Dad learned to surf as a teenager in the 60s. A lifeguard called Malcolm Findlay taught him, "before surfing was cool". He tells me the same tales again and again, but if I could, I'd listen to them forever. I loved those perfect mornings, the two of us and the Beach Boys in the cab of the van. But that particular morning is embedded in my memory. It was the last one we spent surfing. Dad left for the rigs a couple of days later. "Catch you in a fortnight, Scoob," were the last words he said to me.

'Sometimes it feels like it happened to somebody else, and that I'm just telling a story.'

'Yeah. It gets like that when you're older.' I wait for Kelly to cash up the till and do the tips so I can go over to Chris's place.

'You should know.'

'Hey! I'm not *that* old.'

'Keep telling yourself that, *grandad*.'

'I could still run rings around you, *princess*.'

I drain the last of my staff beer; we get one freebie after every shift.

'Sure you could, grandad. Sure you could.' His eyes smile. Kelly has nice eyes.

'Want another?'

'Nah, I better get going. Chris is waiting.'

'Evening of romance ahead, is it?'

'Something like that.'

'Then keep her on her toes, build the anticipation. *Go on.* Have another.' He gives me that look. The one I rarely saw before my surgery. The one I'm still getting used to when I see it on Chris's face. I don't want to like it on Kelly's. But I do. He pops the cap off another Corona and slides the bottle in front of me.

GREGOR: A woman pukes on the person next to her. She's one in the crowd of a hundred or more that're being held back. Everyone is going mental. It's how I imagine the end of the world would look.

'Bill, what's going on?'

'Huh?'

'What's happening here?'

'I…I don't know.' Bill asks a couple of official-looking people. 'Something's gone wrong on the subway. Maybe a tunnel collapsed, or a pipe burst and released toxic fumes. They can't say for sure.' Police are everywhere, trying to keep people in the subway stations.

'Why don't they let them out?'

'I don't know. They might be contaminated.' Two words leap out above the rest. An American guy uses the words "terrorist" and "bomb". The safest country in the world, they said. It's surreal, the panic and the lack of knowing what's going on. The sun keeps rising, which doesn't fit with the slow-motion nightmare going on around us.

The police finally tell the station guards they can let people out onto the streets. And when the crowd pours out, it struggles to breathe.

'Bill, what the hell. Are these people okay? Are they–'

'We need to get you guys back as soon as possible.'

'Where're the ambulances? For Christ's sake, tell me Japan has ambulances.'

'They're coming!' It's the first time Bill's been stressed since we got here. Then, quieter, he says: 'They must be coming.'

The woman from before pukes on the pavement behind me. A TV crew that's appeared from nowhere start to film her, without asking her permission, or if she's okay. All they care about is getting reports on the morning news. I need to help, but what can I do?

'HELP!' I shout at nobody, and then to a lady with a microphone and her cameraman. 'Help these people! Take them to the hospital!' Hordes emerge from the station entrance like something out a zombie film. Their eyes streaming. Sneezing and sniffling and trying not to look up at the sun. I go to the cameraman, who seems like he understands what I'm saying. 'Are more ambulances coming? There're millions of people in this city. A few ambulances aren't enough.' He shrugs and then points the camera at an older man pulling at his tie. The old guy's having a hard time breathing. If this is how the safest, most efficient country on the planet responds to terrorism, then we're all screwed. Nobody has a clue what they're doing.

I shout at Bill to get the driver. But he's trying to get the rest of the group in one place. We've spread out to buy souvenirs on our last day in Japan.

'We need to get you guys back to the hotel,' he says again.

'We're not sick, Bill. Look at these people.' Another guy pukes into a bin, coughing his guts up. He passes out. Subway workers wear paper facemasks. They carry limp bodies out of the station and leave them on the street. They stick them in rows like it's a graveyard. Some of them move, but some don't; dead for all I know. Their faces pale. And everybody just watching. Standing around and watching it all happening.

A few more ambulances, and then the fire brigade arrives. They join the police in stopping folk who were in the subway getting too close to those who weren't. An elderly lady makes it through and approaches me, bawling. She's pointing at her eyes and then out in front, waving her hands about, wailing and desperate for help. She can't see a thing. It's made her blind. Office workers pull off their ties and undo the top buttons of their shirts. Everybody's noses stream like they've got the flu.

Firemen or the army or some kind of government workers turn up in full radioactive gear and gas masks. White and yellow suits with radiation symbols on the back. I'm pretty sure that World War III's started. I don't know who's pissed at Japan or why, but we're officially in a war zone. This is *Japan* for Christ's sake. Atomic bombs have been dropped here, and it's been attacked again. A skinny reporter with a microphone and power suit screeches, trying to push her way closer to the action. When she's waved off, she spots me, a foreigner in the crowd. She shoves her mic in my face like her numbers have come up in the lottery. The sky could rain fire, a nuclear bomb could flatten Tokyo and turn us into scorch marks on the pavement. And she wants a damn interview.

'Please sir, what happen today?'

TRACK 20: LAST DANCE

DAISY: You want to know what happened? I thought you'd've figured it out by now? J and I fell outside into a fizzy, upside down night. I was vain and full of treachery, with Greg passed out in a bathtub less than a mile away. He might as well've been on the moon. I dragged J round the back of that club, full of drink and anger. I wanted to hurt Greg. Hurt him for lying to me all that time. I was going to do it, or at least, I convinced myself that I was.

I tried to give J a look to signal that things could happen if he wanted them to. There'd be no romance, just drunken revenge. But J didn't move. I went to kiss him, and he let me, but I had to prise his mouth open like I'd had to in the tent five years before. Nothing was happening the way it should, and I felt like a numpty. It was embarrassing. He didn't want to come near me. Looking back, I knew even then that J was safe, that nothing could or would happen between us. It's probably why I tried. I put down his coat for us to sit on, and he slumped to the ground with his hands up over his face. He started to cry, J who doesn't cry at anything, saying "sorry" and "I can't" over and over.

‘Ssshhh. It’s okay. Here,’ I said, ‘lie down.’

I told J we were drunk and being stupid. He rolled into a foetus and sobbed with his head on my lap. I rocked him back and forth like a bairn.

‘It’s okay. Nothing happened. We stopped before anything happened.’

‘I hate myself, Daisy.’

He caught me out with that. Unsure what to say, I stroked his hair, shushing him.

Months have passed since that night in Glasgow. It seems like yesterday and a million years if it’s possible to feel so close and distant at the same time. That’s how time works though, isn’t it? A moment can last forever and forever can feel like a moment.

Here I am again. Scotland swapped for Australia. The bins around the back of the nightclub swapped for the surfboards under the cafe. Difference is, Kelly does all the things that J couldn’t.

When I let myself into Chris’s flat, nearly three hours late, she’s sleeping on the couch. She makes this noise when she’s sleeping, like a cartoon goldfish smacking its lips. Deep breath, “puck”. Deep breath, “puck”. Deep breath, “puck”. I sit and listen to her. To my little goldfish. I admire her dark limbs, her thrummy brown hair tied back so I can see her beautiful face. Coolangatta Queen. Merwoman. What we’re doing isn’t right. It isn’t really me. It hurts all over when I imagine saying those words to her after everything she’s done for me since I got here. I ache, thinking about how I’ve repaid her for it. It’s me that starts to cry this time. I’m the one who hates myself.

Chris wakes up, finds me in tears in front of her.

‘What’s happened, Daisy Parker?’

'Chris–' I try to speak, but my sobs are so painful that words won't come out, I shake my head and wail.

JUNAID: The shinkansen suspends me in 225 km/h motion; outside, the world zips past, but inside, time stands still. I get one of those pre-death film roles of the most significant moments in life. But only moments involving Greg. Him knocking Skud on his arse, eating fast food in the *Wimpy* on his ninth birthday, his excitement about his first win of the *Street Fighter* trophy. What the hell was I thinking? Telling these lies? I suppose honesty has never been my strong point. It's not that I want to be dishonest, and it's not that I can't tell the truth. It's that I've spent so much of my life telling lies that honesty has become counterintuitive. I know, I know. The stuff with Daisy in the alley didn't happen the way I said. Did you figure it out or did she tell you? Forget it, it doesn't matter now, does it? Something like this happens, and you realise that your problems aren't problems at all. At the time, I didn't see an alternative. Truth is, I didn't have sex with Daisy, and I didn't have sex with Aileen, and I've never had a girlfriend in my life.

I don't want your sympathy either. Worse things have happened to better people, and they don't let it stop them from getting on with their lives. It's stupid. I'm stupid. That's all. Look where these lies have gotten me. Look where they've gotten Greg. I hope you don't think this means everything I've said is untrue. It's not. I've been faithful to the truth as I remember it. Though I suppose you could argue that some memories get distorted. Once you learn something new, it affects everything that came before. The stories you created for yourself take on different meanings. Ask Greg or Daisy for their versions of these stories, and I'm sure they would be different. I guess there are as many sides to a story as there are people involved.

I burst into the room at the Okura.

A trophy on the coffee table. Greg is the *Temple Warrior* World Champion.

Was?

The toilet flushes.

Is.

He looks as if he's been awake for a year, walks straight past me, unsurprised, and sits on the couch nearest the TV. He hugs his knees.

'Greg.' He says nothing. 'Is everything...are you...?' He looks. He looks away. 'I heard about the trains. But you weren't on a train, right? I mean, you're okay?' He scowls, waits a long time before saying anything. Then:

'You're fine, I take it? Enjoying your time in Japan?' I don't move a muscle, don't say a word. He shakes his head, exhales one of those disbelief-laughs through his nose. I stand there, scared to move. I've never seen him like this. After a few moments, when the atmosphere settles a little, he points at the phone. 'Your mam rang yesterday, to see how everything was going.' I hadn't thought about contacting my parents. 'You should ring her back. This stuff'll be all over the news.'

'What did you tell her?'

'That you shagged Daisy, got into a fight with a pimp, and pissed off on your own in the middle of the night.' He holds my gaze, and I look away first.

'Greg, look, I need to–'

'Phone your mam, J.' Before my brain can decide between the truth and a phone call to my mother, Bill comes in with sandwiches. He's concerned. He talks us through what's been on the news and looks grateful that I'm in the room. He looks at me more than he looks at Greg, puts a hand on my shoulder. He's too shaken about the subway to question where I've been. It all sounds so far fetched. Made up. There's not enough space in my head for it. A cult: "Aum

Shinrikyo". Chemical development and automatic weapons. Some of Japan's brightest young minds from prestigious universities. Bags of chemicals, getaway drivers, and newspapers soaked in poison. Salarymen and office ladies. Sharpened umbrellas. Ordinary people like you and me, on their way to work.

No: our flights have not been cancelled.

Yes: we can still go home.

Back to reality. If that's what it is.

After Bill has gone, I decide to talk to Greg before phoning my mum, but he locks himself in the toilet.

'Greg. I wanted to–. Can you come out of there?'

Nothing.

I wait five minutes, try again. He turns the shower on to drown me out.

Okay, then. Mum first.

I'm not really with it when I get through to mum. I'm still thinking about what I'll say to Greg if he ever comes out of the bathroom. I give listless answers to mum's questions.

No, we were nowhere near the subway.

Yes, Greg's all right.

Yes, he's spoken to his mum.

Yes, I'm sure I'm okay.

But then I have the overwhelming urge to tell her everything. It's not ideal, and it's not face to face, but she'll find out sooner or later. So, I tell her. It doesn't take as long, and it isn't as hard as I expected. She knew and of course she did. She's my mother. She's been the person who didn't turn out the way her family had expected. Who was pushed away because of that. Waves of relief come through the receiver as she tells me that nothing matters to her more than the fact that I'm okay. She doesn't care about the lies I've had to tell. I'm alive, and that's the most important thing, and she will always, always be my mum, no matter what.

When I get off the phone an hour later, Greg's still in the bathroom. I walk in circles around the sofas, wondering if he heard my conversation. The wait is killing me.

I knock.

'Greg? Are you all right?' Nothing. 'Greg…? *Please*. Can you come out here?' He doesn't.

I wait.

And I wait.

And I wait some more.

I get my stuff together and leave.

WISH

TRACK 21: FROM THE EDGE OF THE DEEP GREEN SEA

DAISY: It happened at the school disco. During what had been the worst twelve months of my life. Until that disco, every day was a day for burning buildings down. It was a horrible year to be a pupil at Invergowan Academy. *Especially horrible,* I should say, since any year's a horrible year to be a pupil at Invergowan Academy. I was not a school disco person. I was a shut-up-in-my-room-nodding-to-the-Cure-under-a-nest-of-dyed-hair person. I'd no intention of bopping to pop hits spun by Mr Patterson. But I chummed up to the girls in my registration class and organised to go with them. I was going to wallflower all night, in an ironic protest against popular culture. But I didn't. I went to the school disco for one thing and one thing only. Junaid Jarvis. Life was crap at home, mam was a mess, and I wanted out. If I could combine that with the opportunity to show the boy who didn't kiss me that I was all grown up, then more's the better.

I'd waited over a year for a chance like this, a chance to tell Junaid Jarvis that he was a total dick. But the fact I wanted to confront him shows that I was still hurt, and that I'd probably fancied him all along. That's how it goes at fourteen. Pathetic.

The night stands out for several reasons. First up was that god-awful Madonna song. It blurted out the speakers while the dance club pranced around in pretentious little circles. Sniffing each others' arses and back bending to walk about like crabs. I knew then I was going to hate it, and was ready to leave. The reason I didn't was cause Mr Patterson actually showed a bit of taste. He played 'The Hanging Garden' from the Cure's 1982 album, *Pornography*. He let the full, dark, drum-filled dream play in its entirety. It cleared the vanilla smiles off the dance floor, but the couples all stayed. They stood in each others' arms. Joined at the lips, their heads and hands in different positions with each flash of the strobe. The silhouettes of their embraces flared up in the cloud from the smoke machine. As much as I love that song, I hated every couple out there.

When the smoke cleared, I noticed Cowie making evil eyes at J and his ginger pal. Rumour was that Greg'd shagged Louise 'The Coo' Cowe, offending her modesty in the process. Ironic, seeing as Greg was still a virgin.

The Coo's brother, Cowie, whispered commands to a few of his consort and gave a big nod when Greg and J went outside. I followed, ready to shout "run!" or grab a teacher if the crap hit the fan. First, though, I thought that J would sort it out. He was a black belt. A frightening kung-Fu fighter with lightning fast kicks. Wa. Woo-ha. He'd prove that I was wrong about him the whole time by beating up the boys and winning me over once more.

'Ho, ho, ho. What do we have here?' said Cowie.

Greg made a rubbish joke like "Is it Christmas?" which wasn't going to help his case. Then this cringey exchange happened. The boys went round in circles, from "Come on then" to "I'm right here" to "So am I" and then back to "Come on then". It was tedious. After all that macho crap, they threw punches at the same time. They stumbled about, pushing and pulling at each other. Cowie shouting for help from his mates, Greg shouting for help from J. It wasn't long before Cowie's mates were on top of Greg, kicking into him.

I went running in to get teachers, upset at J for doing nothing to help his pal. But looking back, I knew that the J I was looking at then was a scared, outnumbered kid. I wouldn't have been able to do anything different. The teachers chased Cowie and his mates away. We were then dragged into the wee kitchenette that always smelled of stale cake. Mr Robertson, the P.E. teacher, got a first aid kit.

'Jesus, look at the state of you.'

Greg made this joke then, he said:

'You think this is bad, you should see the other guys.' He paused for effect, 'Not a scratch between them.' I snorted, and he looked at me for what was the first time. He smiled. I felt something in that smile. Something real. Something different from all the fake, secondary school rubbish.

'It's not funny, Mr Buchan,' went Miss Coleman, an English teacher. 'And don't you laugh either, Miss Parker. This is a serious situation, and it won't go unpunished.' Greg kept his eyes on mine, smiling through his cuts and bruises. His eyes aren't human. The iris is blue, but when you look closely, the inside has these wee dots, like electric ripples. Bluer than blue. I held his gaze for as long as I could before Miss Coleman stood between us and started asking for the details. 'Right, you lot. Names.'

Two more parts of the evening make it one to remember. First was the police raid. We were stuck there for hours. Or seemed that way, at least. It was like being at a house party when parents come home early. Music cut, lights up, being told the fun is over. But that feeling changed when police tackled big Davie Simpson to the floor and burst his nose open. Girls screamed, the lot of us patted down by police officers one by one. Every handbag turned inside out. Lo and behold, the Coo had a bag full of Class As.

'That's not mine. You've planted that.'

'Calm down, Miss Cowe.'

'Calm down? Calm down? One of you've just put drugs in my bag, and you're asking me to calm down?' The Coo made a break for it. It took three police to restrain her. The rest of the dealings were with members of the football team. Boys with gold hoops in their ears pointed their faces to the ground. Busted one by one, the cops pulled drugs from their socks and shoes. I clung to Greg. They took about a dozen people away with them. Half the football team, The Coo, and some of her mates. The rest of us were taken out of class and questioned the following week at school. It was in broadsheets and tabloids up and down the country and went on in the local papers for ages. We spoke about it for months afterwards. Skud died that same night. The guy who'd rolled the oregano joints in the tent down the Campull. It felt weird to have kissed somebody that'd died. He was a year older than the three of us. Now he'd be fifteen forever.

J went dark for a long time. I was glad that he was Greg's best pal. I wanted to become his friend. To be there for him.

Greg was what made the disco stand out above everything else. I dropped clues to him about not wanting to be alone; he didn't need to know that I was alone most of the time anyway. But he couldn't take a hint, so I had to increase my bluntness.

'You could ask me to go for a walk if you wanted.'

'Do you want to go for a walk?'

'Okay.'

We went to the beach first. It was November and as dark as dark gets. At that time of year, it's only light between nine in the morning and three in the afternoon. We walked to the end of the promenade, over to a shelter to get out of the wind, and

I kissed the crap out of Gregor Buchan. He was nervous but excitable, and we kissed for what felt like days. Pushing our tongues into the other's mouths as far as they would go.

I was trying to act cool, as if I'd done it all before, knew exactly what I was doing. When he went up for air, I gave him the biggest love bite the world had ever seen. Sucking his neck till it went black and blue. Greg was terrified, and I loved it.

'Let's go back to mine.'

'Okay.'

That was when everything changed. In the moment I wanted us to take each others' virginity. I knew I'd more experience than Greg, and that made me feel in control. I was ready, and it'd be fun to do it, especially cause my mam wouldn't want me to. It'd be a nice big *up yours,* to do it in the house, right under her nose. That'd get her attention. But Mam was drunk and stumbling about the living room. She was at her worst by that point; beyond bad. Trying to drink herself into an early grave, and, credit where credit's due, she was giving it her all. She'd lost her job, went on benefits and drank the money we got from Dad's life insurance. I got myself up for school, I cleaned, I cooked as best I could. She'd go for days without a shower, scream at me for spending money on food for my packed lunch. If I got to the money before she did, then it was loaf and jam, tins of beans, custard and peaches.

It was Greg that made the difference. And without that disco, there would've been no Greg. Without Junaid Jarvis and the Campull, there'd've been no disco. Everything happens for a reason. It was a messy night, but Greg didn't seem to care. I told him to go home, but he didn't. Then I tried to get him to sleep with me.

'Let's wait a bit,' he said. I thought that was going to be the end of it, figuring that the state of my mam had put him off forever. But it's Greg, so the opposite happened.

He invited me to his house all the time. We walked Lumpy, got fish suppers from the chip shop, played *Mario* on the Nintendo. We did homework and I often "missed" the last bus home, so I had to stay over. I knew he'd told his parents all about it, but they never said anything, never treated me like a charity case. I'd "sleep in the spare room," but didn't spend a full night in there in all those years we were together. I'd slip into Greg's bed, and we'd cling to each other. We took our time. Sex finally happened on the 24th of April 1992, and by then we'd both figured out exactly how everything was supposed to work.

The Buchan house was a sanctuary. His mam and dad liked me, thought I was good for their son, and I became part of the family.

Mam got worse during that year, and according to her, it was my fault. Her daughter wasn't there to take care of her grieving mother.

'What about me?'

'He was *my husband*!'

'He was my dad! Don't blame your crap on me not being here. Where were you? I was a bairn! I needed a mam! Where were you at?'

'Don't you dare speak to me like that!'

I don't know how many times we had that argument. A lot. At fifteen, she kicked me out the house. I stayed at Greg's for two months.

He went round to my house without telling me. To try and speak sense into my mam. 'Is this what you want? Daisy living with another family? You want to lose her as well?' It wasn't as easy as all that, but I'll spare the details. I've been rambling too much. But understand that Greg brokered the peace treaty. He called Mam "Mrs P", told her jokes. He'd rent films and suggest we watch them together. There were some nights that didn't feel like all was lost. And then there were more of them.

He'd get her to gang up on me about my love of Robert Smith and the Cure. If we went out to the shops, he'd ask if she needed anything. They sound like little things. But sometimes little things are really big things. Mam started to get better, not exactly her old self, but better, and I moved back into the house.

The school disco was where it started. That's what I was telling you about. We put my mam to bed, made a nest, and listened to *Pet Sounds* on Scratchy the turntable. And all these years later, after everything, I came home. How could I not?

WILD MOOD SWINGS

TRACK 22: NUMB

GREGOR: That was the day the world changed. Have you had one of those? When there's a clear break in the life from before and the one that comes after. I'm lucky if I make it through a day without bursting into tears. Those are good days. Bad days are dark, even if it's bright outside.

I keep reading this poem by Wilfred Owen. It came back to me when I got home from Japan. We did it in third year at school. I didn't have a clue what Wilfred was on about back then. I went to the library and hunted it down, copying it and a few others into a notebook. It's called *Dulce et decorum est*. It means "How sweet and decorous it is". Did you do it at school as well? It's a poem about the trenches in World War I that makes a lot more sense to me since Japan.

There's this attack, where the writer's squad gets hit with gas shells. When I first read the poem years ago, I imagined it happening at night. Now I imagine it in the daytime. Like the subway. Why do we think that bad things can't happen during the day? They can. They do. In the poem, the men shout and stumble about, drowning in a "green sea". One guy gets caught bad, his "white eyes writhing in his face". I laughed at that when I was at school. I don't think it's funny anymore. Wilfred wrote this other poem called *Mental Cases*. We didn't read this one in English class. It's about these guys coming home from war, and there's this one line that I keep coming back to. It says, "Dawn breaks open like a wound that bleeds afresh". Reading that line is the closest thing I've had to a feeling since I got home. A sentence from a dead poet. The book said he was killed in the war, a week before it ended. He was twenty-five.

Doesn't end though, does it, Wilfred?

Dawn breaks open like a wound that bleeds afresh. That's how dawn feels for me now. I don't open the curtains. I'd rather have the black. Live in it, as if days don't pass. Because if days don't pass then we can't hurt each other. I try to play games, to use the VX0 my mam got me to try and "cheer me up", but my concentration's non-existent. Most days I don't even get out of bed. When I do, and it's rare, I try to go out. I walk Lumpy, but it's so I can get away from my mam, who buzzes around as though nothing's happening and nothing's changed.

Everything's changed.

Can't she see?

Can't you?

DAISY: For my sixteenth birthday present, we went to see the Cure. It was a few months before I actually turned sixteen; they were touring to promote the album *Wish*. The gig was at the Barrowland Ballroom in Glasgow. I freaked out when Greg told me we were going. I had no idea he'd bought tickets, and will never forget the date–the 24th of April, 1992.

So off we went; me, Greg, and our mothers! Can you imagine? If you told me I'd be at a Cure concert with my mam before I met Greg Buchan, I'd've laughed in your face. But there we were. Got the train down and stayed in a Holiday Inn. Greg was supposed to be in a room with his mam, and me in a room with mine. But they let us share, unaware (or not) at how much we'd already shared a bed. It was our first time, though, and by the time we met our mams for breakfast, we'd fit in our second time too.

At the concert, we left our mothers alone to plan our non-existent future wedding (or whatever they did that night). Greg pushed us to the front, put me on his shoulders and I spent the whole gig trying to catch Robert Smith's eye. At the start of the encore, before he sang 'Three Imaginary Boys,' he did more than just look at me; he smiled. *Robert Smith.* Smiled right at me. I was not-quite-sixteen and, after Dad, didn't think that kind of happiness was ever going to be possible for me again.

Just like I thought I'd never surf, or go to Australia without Dad.

JUNAID: Mum and Dad pick me up at the train station. Mum's smile is spread across her face as she wraps me up in a warm hug. Dad focusses his eyes anywhere but on mine as he gives me a job-interview handshake. Mum hits him in the chest when he doesn't offer to take my bag. I insist that I can manage, but she makes him carry it to the car. I get in the seat behind dad so that Mum can stare at me from the front passenger's side. We get a lunch of fish and chips on the way out of Aberdeen, stopping down the beachfront to eat it. Mum asks thousands of questions about Japan and shakes her head in disbelief at the answers. She asks me to say something in Japanese, and I tell her that her roots need dying. She cracks up when I translate what I've said.

It's an hour's drive to Cairn Bay, our sleepy North-East village. I expect to spend the whole trip worrying about what's going to happen next, but then I notice it. It's on the floor behind mum's seat. A *Kays* catalogue.

And that makes me relive the whole thing.

He was a model, so his whole career revolved around being attractive. Luscious black curls on head and chest, muscled shoulders and slender hips. He had it all, including the arrogant, brooding poses. He was a professional at the "point-into-the-distance" pose when displaying active wear. Not to mention the "I'm-honestly-playing-football" pose when clad head to toe in the latest kit. My personal favourite was the "come-to-bed" eyes used when he modelled underwear. "Julio", as I'd affectionately named my first crush, could be found for years in the pages of *Kays*.

My pals' fantasies came from the stockings and bras in the *Women's Lingerie* section. I preferred to dip into the *Men's Underwear* pages. I imagined that Julio lived in the cupboard where I hid the catalogue that aided my daydreams. He was from a village in Spain (or sometimes Brazil). Julio had to hide his sexuality too. Those in the Catholic mountains of Spain/Brazil believed that the devil sent homosexuals to destroy humanity.

Sometimes he was an exchange student and I'd be assigned to help improve his language. Under the desks in the library, he'd run his hand up my thigh, suggesting he come to mine for Supper. He'd win Mum over with his smile and Dad with his knowledge of sports. He'd wink at my old man after giving him a tip for Sunday football. Then we'd head up to my room to play loud music because it helped us "study". And boy would we "study". We'd "study" until we were all "studied" out.

And those were my thoughts as I poured over the *Kays* before bed. As some people pray before going to sleep, so I prayed at the altar of Julio. The thick catalogue, open like a Bible, lay propped on a pillow before me as I kneeled, naked, on the floor. I'd performed this act of worship many times. And that's how Dad caught me, coming into my room to pass on a message from Mum that I never got to hear. I glimpsed the shock on his face. I closed the catalogue, rushing to cover myself with the pillow that propped it up. Dad hadn't seen me naked in years. He didn't hit me. Nothing like that. He just picked up the catalogue and left the room.

He hasn't mentioned it since.

GREGOR: There's a shadow in this room. He's been here a while. I try to ignore him, but he doesn't care. He just sits there. Sometimes on the couch. Sometimes on the desk. Sometimes he lies right next to me in bed. You deserve your hurt, he says. Stop running. You should feel it. Shouldn't you? Because you're worthless. Pathetic. Stop blaming others for your own BS. You did this. You brought this on yourself. *Pathetic.* A crappy son, a pointless boyfriend, people moving to other countries to get away from you. You're garbage.

I go to the bathroom for a tissue. Nobody else is home. I blow my nose. Feel something in my left eye. An eyelash. I look in the mirror, pull down the bottom lid, but the eyelash is nowhere to be seen. I look at my eyeball. The veins. The iris. Then he's in there with me. The shadow. He's over my right shoulder, and he gives me a suggestion. A wee nudge towards what I should do if I want to feel better. I look again at my eye, pull down the lid. The knife with the wooden handle would slot in there without too much effort. A wee push.

I know exactly where it is in the kitchen.

TRACK 23: RETURN

JUNAID: Far out over the beach, the world ends. Miles of empty coastline winds its way from the village to the nearby towns. About a mile from Cairn Bay, the coast curves round to an inlet that connects the North Sea to the Loch of Strathbeg. Because it slices through the beach, we call this little channel the "Cut". I call the area beyond the Cut "The End of the World". This is because of the flaming towers of St. Fergus gas terminal in the distance. You almost never meet other people when you walk on this part of the beach, and for that reason, I've done it often. Countless teenage angsty trips.

As kids, we imagined the terminal was a post-apocalyptic fort to be stormed. The blaze above St. Fergus giving that end-of-world feel. As well as towers of fire, an aerodrome of thirty antenna masts lies between the Loch of Strathbeg and the gas terminal. The masts at Crimond Aerodrome still belong to the Ministry of Defence, though the surrounding land is owned by farmers. Remnants of the Cold War, each of the masts are strapped to the earth by a dozen heavy duty cables. The cables stretch from ever higher points, off the structures and down to weighted pulleys further and further out on the ground.

These allow the masts to stay up, but also to sway in high winds. The masts served as an early warning system for the US, there to detect nukes should the USSR launch them. Nearby Mormond Hill, on the horizon to the west, was hollowed out and used as a control tower. Legend has it that the Americans filled it in with cement when they left, leaving all the equipment inside. We did a project on it at school. There's no reason to know all this stuff.

The iron landscape is made more dramatic by the loss of sun, white and quiet behind a never-ending blanket of cloud. Parts are such a deep grey that they're almost purple. A steam-punk-zeppelin cloud makes its way over the closest mast, but the blanket above my head doesn't move. It hangs there, stuck to the sky. The evening wind gives a chill: it might be the end of the Earth after all.

I'm the only person out on the beach. Last man standing. There's half an hour of sunlight left, it's definitely too late and too cold for others to walk this far over today. The closest mast seems to call out, so the ninja in me decides to climb it.

The antenna is massive. I'd guess ninety feet high. After crossing two fences to get to the base of it, there's a sign that reads:

MoD PROPERTY
KEEP OUT

The next fence has a sign with a black and yellow triangle. Inside the triangle, a man on his back is being struck with a bolt of lightning:

DANGER OF DEATH
High Voltage

Climbing it is stupid. Not least because it's trespassing and there's the chance of death by giant bolts of lightning. But with the sun going down and the wind picking up, why would anyone want to be up an antenna at the end of the Earth?

I'm in the middle of the triangular structure. Diagonal girders could be climbed, but in the centre of the mast is a convenient ladder. This tells me that at one time or another, these were meant to be ascended, so touching it isn't going to induce the wrath of Thor. I take a few breaths with my foot poised on rung number one. A cow looks at me over the outer fence, tilting its head as it chews the cud. I don't stop to look, I climb and climb, one rung after the other. About a quarter of the way up, a gust of wind makes the whole thing shake. I look up at the top of the mast, it's swaying.

I wait for the swaying to calm down before going any further. But I do. About halfway up there's a kind of platform which I sit on, still clinging to the ladder, so I'm not blown off. I take in the view. Fields spread out to my left, and the beach is to my right. I look for the sprinkle of houses that makes up Cairn Bay. But with daylight struggling to cling to the sky and the streetlights not yet on, all I can make out is a grey spludge. The view is a near empty canvas of green-brown fields and the blue-black expanse of the North Sea. It's the opposite of Tokyo.

Another gust of wind rocks the antenna, and I cling while the mast sways up top. Far below, the cow moos. Today was the first time I've seen my parents since I told my mum. Tomorrow'll be the first time I've seen Daisy since Aileen's house party. I haven't seen Greg since he hid from me in the Okura, months ago. I stayed in Japan as long as I could after Greg left, just like Daisy decided to stay in Australia. In the end, none of us made it to university. I haven't even made it back to Kyoto yet, enrolling in a language school in Tokyo.

Bill's been amazing. He helped me find a place to stay, sorted out my visas and told me about the school, where I study Japanese five hours a day. I decided to forgo Business Studies and applied for a Japanese degree instead. I'll attend a university in Tokyo starting in April, the beginning of the Japanese school year. Bill says he'll be able to help me find a job or at least get me an internship at Irata after I graduate. But I haven't thought that far ahead. I wanted to stay in Japan, get as much Japanese study done as I could before I start uni, but it was my fault; I had to come back.

I take one last look at the view before making my descent. The only vibrancy is the purple in the clouds and the fire that spills from the gas works behind me. The exposed landscape is beautiful in its own way, but with the overcast sky above, is as bleak as I've ever seen it.

GREGOR: The doctor's hopeful that he's saved my eye. We won't know until he takes the blindfold off, and I'm to leave the thing on as long as possible. If one eye goes, it can take the other with it, so I'm in darkness. Ironic, seeing as I can't imagine a future. I can't see past the next sunset, the next meal, the next breath. It's empty space. Black.

I'm not hearing voices, if that's what you think. That stuff about the shadow, it was more like a presence was in the room with me, a force I couldn't control. But then when I say that out loud, I can hear how mental I sound.

'What can I do, Greg. What can I do here?'

'Nothing. This conversation for the umpteenth time isn't helping.'

'I'm your mother, and I didn't see it coming.'

'It's not your fault, Mam. You can read me another letter. You can do that.'

Daisy went quiet for a while, but then she started up posting stuff again. I haven't replied to a single letter. And until Mam started reading them to me, I hadn't read any of them either. So, in a way, Daisy was writing to nobody. Putting thoughts in envelopes and sending them out into nothing. I'd no plans to ever read what she sent, especially after Japan, but then this happened. Mam changed my bed sheets when I came into the hospital and found the unopened letters under my mattress. I'm not allowed to be left alone, because I'm "high risk". So, this is what we do to pass the time.

I argued to start with, but I was soon taken in by the timeline of her story. I think about Daisy a lot, but I was so far off the mark about what was going on in Australia. The first letters still sound like Daisy. She writes about her mam and dad. How it's coming up for the anniversary of his death, and she wants to surf again to commemorate him. She doesn't tell anybody she used to surf. She swapped wetsuits for fishnets and hid behind a Robert Smith hairdo. She thanks me for being her "first real relationship", said she was sorry how it turned out in the end, the mess it left. She doesn't want to give up on us being friends and is desperate to see Lumpy if she "ever comes home for a visit".

Mam laps it up. She says things like "oh, listen to this, Greg" and "did you hear that, Greg? She got that job, good on her". She supports her surrogate daughter's travel and surfing. I'm not as upset as I thought I'd be hearing about Daisy's new life, but then, I haven't felt much of anything for months. My mam cried when the nurse sat us down to explain the situation with my eye. I just sat there. Does it make any difference if it works or not? Does it make any difference if I can or can't see? Would the world be any worse off if I wasn't even here?

The writing becomes love letters to surfing and the sea, and Mam starts to get into the story of it. "She can paint a bonny picture, Greg, can't she?" I spend half the time calculating, always asking what date each letter is so I can feed it into the timeline. What was Daisy up to when I was on the plane to

Japan? How about when I was in a terrorist war zone? Or standing in the toilet with a shadow at my back? Daisy "had to go and be on her own", to "find herself", figure out the "person that she wants to be". The word selfish springs to mind. Running away doesn't solve problems. I thought I could leave mine in Japan, but they made their way to the other side of the world. If hers didn't follow her to Australia, they'll be waiting when she gets back. Ha! Listen to me. The guy who stuck a knife in his face. I've got all the answers, don't I? Don't *eye*. I can pun too.

JUNAID: I don't recognise her right away. She's almost as brown as I am, her hair short and swishing about her shoulders. She walks different, starts to run when she spots me. I open my arms to catch her as she leaps up and wraps her legs around my waist.

'Daisy Parker. As I live and breathe.'

'Junaid Jarvis. Genki desu ka?'

'Genki, genki. Hisashiburi desune?'

'Okay, okay, I only learned "how's it going?" so you'll have to stick to the Queen's.'

'I said, "long time no see". You're prettier than ever.'

'Thanks. You don't look too shabby yourself.'

'So. Tell me everything.'

We walk over the beach, wrapped in layer upon layer of jumpers and jackets, hats and scarves. We talk about Oz, about how she's trying to make up her mind whether to come home or go back out there. She speaks about surfing, about her job and the people that make up her social circle. I tiptoe around anything involving Greg, our fight in Japan and his accident. I tell her all the positive stuff first.

It's good to catch up. To see someone that I've known for so long. Someone I don't have to think too hard to be around.

It's as if the party at Aileen's might've been a week ago. But we've met to do more than catch up. I have wrongs to right.

'It's my fault, Daize.'

'What is?'

'Greg. It's my fault.'

'How can it be your fault? It was an accident.'

'Accident? What did his mam say happened?'

'About the crash. After that stuff in Japan with the poison gas, what kind of crappy luck do you need to–'

'It was no accident, Daize. There wasn't any crash.'

She searches my face for an explanation.

'What do you mean?'

'Greg. He did it to himself.'

Nora told me it was an accident too. She wanted me to come home, but I told her that I wouldn't be coming back until after my first term at university. I couldn't afford to go home twice.

'That's not good enough, Junaid,' she said. 'He needs to be surrounded by his friends right now. If you love him, you'll come home. Please, Junaid, come home.' I still resisted. I'd be back later in the year, I'd see him soon enough. 'He might not be here later in the year!' I'd never heard Nora so upset. 'He did it to himself, Junaid. I don't know what else he might do.'

She told me then. Plainly. Simply.

He'd been operated on. They weren't sure if the eye was saved or not, though it was looking hopeful. But Greg wasn't himself, and the hospital advised having somebody with him round the clock. They're scared he might do it again, go further.

'Christ,' says Daize.

'It gets worse. And I don't know how you're going to take this.'

'Take what?'

'In Japan. We had a fight. A bad one. I left him alone in Tokyo. I went back after I heard about the subway, but he wouldn't speak to me. He locked himself in the bathroom at the hotel. Stayed in there. Turned the shower on when I tried to talk through the door. He thinks we...'

'He thinks we what?'

'He thinks we had sex. In Glasgow. That night of the competition.'

'Why does he think that?'

'Because I told him that's what happened.'

'For Christ's sake, J. Why would you say that?'

'I don't know. It was a weird situation. He was moody, didn't want to leave the hotel in the first place. And we got into a stupid argument, and he brought that up again. I was being sarcastic, but I don't think he took it that way. And we'd got into a bit of an altercation with these pimps–'

'Pimps?'

'It's not like it sounds, we weren't–I'm not doing a good job of this. We'd been for noodles and it was near the red light district, and these pimps were hassling us to buy prostitutes and that turned into Greg and I having a scuffle, but then it turned into this full-blown war of words, I went too far, wanted to hurt him, it came to blows in the end, and the things we said to each other, it was a mistake, it was, I don't know... *Absurd.*' I run out of steam. I don't know how else to say it. She doesn't speak for a while. Just looks out to the horizon as I watch everything play out across her sober face.

'So, what can we do?'

'Tell the truth. Make it right. I'm finished with lies, Daize. I've been lying all my life.' She nods, still trying to process it all.

'Okay.'

GREGOR: 'Both of them?'

'Aye. Both of them.'

'And how do they know I'm in hospital?'

'Greg. This is Junaid you went to primary school with. Daisy. Daisy who lived in our house, Daisy. How do you *think* they know? I *told* them.' Mam's on the verge of tears.

'I don't want *him* in here. I'm not sure I want *her* in here either.'

'Why would you say that? These are your *friends*, Gregor.'

'*Were*, Mam. You don't know the half of it.'

'They've come all the way across the world to see you. Maybe it's time to put differences aside.'

'I'm not ready, Mam.'

'Okay, sweetheart.' Footsteps. Door. 'Come on in you two.'

'Mam!'

'Greg. Daisy and Junaid are here to see you. Isn't that nice? They've come all the way from Japan and Australia. Must've cost them a fortune.' Massive pause before Mam continues. 'Well. I'll leave you all to catch up.'

Footsteps.

Door.

Silence.

DAISY: Greg's in a bed wearing superhero pyjamas, the top half of his head wrapped in a bandage. Cotton wooly stuff pokes out of it. He won't be able to see us, and that's easier, for the time being. I realise that I don't know which eye is the one he–I don't know which eye has the problem. His beard is scraggly and untrimmed, his hair long. He must've been growing it since I left.

J tries first.

'Greg, I–'

'Get out. I don't want you here. I didn't ask for this.'

'Greg, please–'

'GET OUT!'

I try next.

'Greg, J needs to tell you someth–'

'That you shagged him? He's spilt those beans already, Daize.'

'Greg! We never did anything like that.'

'Aye, right. A big joke was it? Hilarious, guys.'

'For Christ's sake, Greg. This is J we're speaking about. Do you really think–'

'OUT! I don't want to hear it, right? I don't want anything to do with either of you again.' He gets up. Right up out of the bed and throws a pillow at where he thinks we're standing. J reaches out and catches it, then tries again.

'Greg, listen to me–'

'OUT! Get the hell out! What part of "out" do you not–'

'I'M GAY YOU GINGER WANKER! I'M GAY. HEAR ME? GAY, GAY, GAY, GAY, GAY, GAY, GAY!' He flings the pillow back at Greg, and it thumps into his chest.

JUNAID: There. I said it. *Finally.* Dad's struggling with the whole thing, retreated to the garden shed and been in there since. I hope you're not going to be weird too. I mean, you knew all along, right? Saw it coming? Good. Now it's official. I'm "out". Go and gossip to your pals about it if you want. I don't care anymore.

I'm past caring.

The Skud thing. That's what did it. That's what made me call my mum from Japan and tell her. That night at the Campull, when we played spin the bottle–he was scared. Scared I'd out him. Tell our secret. The way he kissed that girl, Lisa. Made a show of touching her. That was for me. To let me know he was off bounds. I realised later that I wasn't upset about Lisa; I was jealous of her. I know that might sound stupid, but it was like he was rejecting me. Throwing our secret back in my face. I forgave him for doing that because now I understand why he had to. But back then, I couldn't figure it out.

The reason he turned people against me, for what happened in the tent, that the last thing he did was protect me–it was all because he saw me for what I was. For who I am. And he knew I'd be able to see it in him too.

I've lied for the best part of two decades. To my family, to my friends, to myself. Even when I knew I was lying, it was easier to keep lying than face the truth. Skud always told me never to tell anyone, and you can see why. My dad isn't exactly happy about having a gay son. Why you say? It's the twentieth century, and no one cares if you're gay anymore? Ha! Where do *you* live? Thailand? San Fransisco? Try living in a fishing village in the North East of Scotland. Try being gay here. Count how many people are willing to come out in Scottish fishing villages.

Jesus.

Try being gay in Japan. I don't know how I'd begin to navigate that if it weren't for Bill. But that doesn't matter. Where I live doesn't matter.

I went to Skud's grave the other day. He's in the cemetery in Invergowan, in the newer bit at the back. His stone took me a while to find because it doesn't say Skud on it. It says his name. Kenneth Kilpatrick.

Junaid Jarvis. Kenneth Kilpatrick.

We used to laugh about that like it meant something. As if we were meant to find each other. He'd call me "Pinglish" in front of other people, but "Jun" when we were alone. Like the two different "Skuds" I knew, there were also two different versions of Junaid Jarvis. "Skud" and "Pinglish" were people who went to the same school, who might bump shoulders in the corridor. But in stolen glances and secret moments, we were Jun and Kenny.

I stood at his grave, but I wouldn't allow tears to form in

my eyes.

Sorry, Kenny, but I can't lie anymore.

It's time to break my promise.

GREGOR: 'That's right. I'm gay. Daisy knows. She's known for a while. We never slept together. I don't know why I said that. Actually, I do know, I said it to hurt you, and I'm sorry. I'm sorry, Greg. About your eye. It's my fault. I know I'm the reason you–'

'Gay?'

'Yup.'

'Aye,' says Daize 'He's a–'. A snicker. A childish snicker. Then it turns into a snort. That's Daisy Parker laughing if ever I've heard it.

'Are you dickbags laughing? You better not be laughing.'

'No,' she says. Swallowing it, and then I can hear J at it as well, holding in a laugh.

'What, exactly, is so funny?'

'J,' says Daize. 'You thought we…and he's a–', but she can't get the word out.

I say "homosexual" and they crack up. 'You pair are mental.'

'Remember Aileen Hendry's party? Before I went to Australia? I caught him and Cowie at it in a room full of Barbies!'

'Hey!' says J, 'he loved it.' Daisy bursts. My brain struggles to compute what I'm hearing. *J's gay? Cowie?*

'And you,' it's Daisy again. 'You can't see them, but you're wearing kids' pyjamas!'

'With,' says J, 'Spiderman!' The word "Spiderman" is so high pitched I can barely make it out.

They howl.

'Piss off. I like Spiderman.'

They roar.

TRACK 24: THE 13TH

DAISY: J told me back in Glasgow. He went all shy. Spoke about being confused, about how he was "maybe attracted to guys". He made this joke about boys wanting to beat him up and nothing else. But he was half-serious. Afraid people could see it when he was too scared to say it out loud.

Greg's blind.

But only in one eye. The one he–

It's the left eye.

He's decided to opt for an eye patch. Obviously. It's Greg, after all. A man who wears cowboy boots. The eye patch completes his look. I told him that. He said, "it does, doesn't it?"

We all sat in his room at the Buchan house, playing Zelda and Donkey Kong and Mario Kart. Nora'd bring in mugs of tea and plates of McVitie's Chocolate Digestives. I said nothing about Chris or Kelly, sticking to surfing if I said anything at all. Most nights I just sat with Lumpy and watched the boys. Watched them battle their way through magic and mysterious worlds. I thought about what it would be like to live in those worlds. Where magic potions bring people back to life. And, if you mess up, all you've to do is jump off a cliff to go back to the last save point. The last point where things were good. It gets better, Greg gets better, but he's never as bright as when we played video games back in the early days.

We've made up about as much as is possible under the circumstances. He opened up a bit about the terrorist attack, how it affected him. He read us these old poems from school. He doesn't blame J, or me, or the terrorists. He says he could've asked for help, could've got out of the dark room, but when it was happening it seemed impossible. He's getting there. A day at a time.

As for me, I wasn't sure what road to go down next, but then I had a dream about Silvia's fig tree. It was the highest fig tree in the universe, and I was hanging from it. I had to choose a fig, but if I let go to grab one, I would've fallen. The weird thing was that my arms were really long and my feet near touched the ground. But still all I could think of was falling; *failing*. I woke up then, and I knew that I was going to university in London.

I'm done at Kelly's, and who knows if Chris'll ever speak to me again. I'll join the surf club and get over to Cornwall at weekends, read novels on the train on the way there. One day, I'll write my own. Write out all this stuff with Greg and J. Give each of them their chance to tell their story, name each chapter of the book after a Cure album. I'll get things wrong and make mistakes. Maybe I won't quite capture the essence of Greg's resolve or the transformation of J from village 'loon' to Tokyoite. But I'll do my best. I've no idea if it'll work out, but that's what I've decided on for now. Most people stare at the tree, too scared to pick a fig for fear of missing out on the others. I've decided that taking a chance on one of the figs is better than no fig at all.

JUNAID: I head out towards the beach. I walk halfway to the Cut, let the surf lap at my feet. I've stepped into the sea at all times of the year. She's cold. In winter, she's so cold that she can kill you in three minutes. Once, in December, I ran into her as a dare. But that was about three seconds, not three minutes. I can't believe Daize used to surf in this.

Tomorrow I leave for Japan to start my course. I've spent the last month with friends and family before moving over. I hung out with Daize a lot; she's promised to come visit at some point. I also put in lots of time with Mum, but more than anyone, I spent time with Greg. He wears an eyepatch now, calls himself the "Captain". We went through a couple days on each of the old consoles, digging out our favourite games from years gone by. He's doing so much better, better than my dad is, I'd say. He spends half his time on his virtual reality thing. Still talks about using it to take over the world.

The tide's in. The sun's a glint on the horizon. I take off all my clothes and wade until the sea is up to my knees. It's freezing. I throw a few splashes onto my body, and it brightens my eyes. When I'm in up to my waist, I dive under to get it over with. My skin goes tight around frozen bones, and I blow a spray of water from my mouth, tasting the salt on my lips. I know I won't last long, so I wade out to chest level, walking my legs and breast-stroking my arms. Inhalations become shaky, exhalations forceful. I bury my feet in the sand and let the pulse of the North Sea rock me. My veins pop. I'm alive. A living, breathing, *feeling* human being.

The sea pulls me back and forth with the roll of her waves. I get used to the motion, weighing up the bottle in my hand. I move into the best throwing position I can. On the next wave that scoops me to and then from the shore, I sling the bottle in the general direction of Japan. It plunks down into the water.

'I'll race you.'

GREGOR: Master Plans change. That's what I've learned. They have to adapt. I've had to adapt to Daisy leaving, to J coming out. To having one eye with which to kick the crap out of him at *Street Fighter*.

I'm doing okay.

That is, I've got no desire to put sharp instruments into my body. That's a start. The shadow's gone most days, and when he rears his ugly head, I'm getting better at fighting him off. I'll tell you what's helped: *Second Self*.

That's the name of my virtual world.

I've been developing it. It's given me something to focus on. A light at the end of the tunnel. And I know you keep up with technology, so if you haven't heard of the Internet yet, then you've been living in a cave. Our house was the first in the village to get online. The possibilities are endless.

Imagine.

People from all over the world could connect in *Second Self*. It'll be a fully realised universe that lasts as long as you do. People'll meet, hang out, make pals. They'll go on dates, fall in love, they'll even get married. Virtually. They'll create things together, exchange ideas and experiences.

They'll help each other.

In the not too distant future, we'll all have *Second Selves*.

We'll all have second chances.

JAPANESE WHISPERS

TRACK 25: KYOTO SONG

AIKO: Many years ago, I worked at a Kaleidoscope museum in Kyoto. I met a Scottish boy called Junaid there once. He wasn't what I expected a Scottish person to look or sound like. He was scruffy and hungover, but I felt for him. Junaid-san was lost. I was young, but I could see that much. He needed a friend. Someone to give him direction, or to be there as he figured out the directions for himself. We read my favourite children's story, about a dragonfly named "Light". Then I sent him up a mountain to sweat out his booze and clear his head.

His friend was caught up in the devastating Aum Shinrikyo subway attack. I remember the trip to the train station to put Junaid-san on the shinkansen to Tokyo. I still think about it sometimes. I hope that Junaid-san managed to write his own ending, that he finally understood the lesson of the book. If we write our own life stories, then we also have the power to choose our own endings.

If a simple bug can transform into a dragonfly, imagine what you could do.

ACKNOWLEDGMENTS

My sincere thanks go to everyone who played a part in making this book what it is. First and foremost I have to thank my wife and son, Diane and Lewis, for making me a better human being.

Similarly, gratitude and love go to my parents for allowing me to pursue my passions.

Thanks must also go to Yvonne de Graaf for the room, Libby Peatman for the job and the University of Kent for the library, which is where I wrote most of this manuscript.

More thanks to Emily Bryson for always being my first and best reader, Norma Fores for the Barcelona retreat and to Luke Palfreeman and Bill O'Connor for their help during my "research" trips to Japan.

Finally, thank you to Chris Kelso and Euan Kilpatrick for all of the emotional (and financial) support over the years, and for Disneyland.

ABOUT THE AUTHOR

Michael Milton is a writer from Aberdeenshire, Scotland. His short stories have been long and short listed for the Fish Prize, the Bath Short Story Award, the Mogford Prize and the Emerge Impact Creative Writing Prize. He holds an MA in Creative Writing from the University of Kent.

Kissing Daisy Parker is his first novel, and yes, he can beat you at *Street Fighter*.

facebook.com/mikemiltonbooks
twitter.com/mikemiltonbooks
instagram.com/mikemiltonbooks

Printed in Great Britain
by Amazon

44873550R00144